# Birds of Colorado

### Todd Telander

**FALCON**GUIDES

GUILFORD, CONNECTICUT
HELENA, MONTANA

AN IMPRINT OF GLOBE PEQUOT PRESS

To my wife, Kirsten, my children, Miles and Oliver, and my parents, all of whom have supported and encouraged me through the years. Special thanks to Mike Denny for his expert critique of the illustrations.

To buy books in quantity for corporate use or incentives, call **(800) 962-0973** or e-mail **premiums@GlobePequot.com**.

FSC
www.fsc.org

MIX
Paper from responsible sources
FSC® C005010

# FALCONGUIDES®

Copyright © 2012 Morris Book Publishing, LLC
Illustrations © Todd Telander

FalconGuides is an imprint of Globe Pequot Press.
Falcon, FalconGuides, and Outfit Your Mind are registered trademarks of Morris Book Publishing, LLC.

Library of Congress Cataloging-in-Publication Data is available on file.

ISBN 978-0-7627-7418-0

Printed in the United States of America

10 9 8 7 6 5 4 3 2 1

# Contents

## Nonpasserines

# Passerines

# Introduction

Colorado is a region of extremes. The great Rocky Mountains include the Continental Divide, which runs down the state's center and separates the vast Great Plains on the east from the high, arid plateaus to the west. This geographic diversity provides for an incredible variety and number of bird species, and gives birders a unique opportunity to see western and eastern birds of North America whose ranges intersect here. From high-altitude tundra, montane parks, grasslands, river canyons, and desert sage lands, Colorado supports habitat for resident breeders and seasonal visitors, as well as those passing through on migration to and from South America and Canada. This guide describes the most common birds you are likely to encounter here and includes some that are only found in this area.

# Notes about the Species Accounts

## Order

The order of species listed in this guide is based on the latest version of the *Checklist of North American Birds,* published by the American Ornithologist's Union. In an effort to remain current, I have used the most recent arrangement, so the arrangement of some groups, especially within the nonpasserines, may be slightly different than that of older field guides.

## Names

For each entry I have included the bird's common name as well as the scientific name. Since common names tend to vary regionally, or there may be more than one common name for each species, the universally accepted scientific name of genus and species (such as *Nucifraga columbiana* for Clark's Nutcracker) is a more reliable identifier. Also, you can often learn interesting facts about a bird from the English translation of its Latin name. For instance, the term Nucifraga derives from the Latin *nucis,* meaning "nut," and *fraga,* meaning "to break."

## Families

Birds are grouped into families based on similar traits, behaviors, and genetics. When trying to identify an unfamiliar bird, it is often helpful to first place it into a family, which will limit your search to a smaller group. For example, if you see a long-legged, long-billed bird lurking in the shallows, you can begin your search in the family group of Ardeidae (Herons and Egrets), and narrow your search from there.

## Size

The size listed for each bird is the average length from the tip of its bill to the end of its tail, if the bird was laid out flat. Sometimes females and males vary in size, and this is mentioned in the text. Size can be misleading if you are looking at a small bird that happens to have a very long tail or bill. It may be more effective to use the bird's relative size, or judge the size difference between two or more species.

## Season

The season provided in the accounts is when the greatest number of individuals occur in Colorado. Some species are year-round residents that breed here. Others may spend only summers or winters in the state, and some may be transient, only stopping during migration in the spring or fall. Even if only part of the year is indicated for a species, be aware that individuals may arrive earlier or remain for longer than the given time frame. Plumage also changes with the season for many birds, and this is indicated in the text and illustrations.

## Habitat

A bird's habitat is one of the first clues to its identification. Note the environment where you see a bird and compare it to the description listed. This can be especially helpful when identifying a bird that shares traits with related species. For example, Cattle Egrets and Snowy Egrets are similar, but Cattle Egrets are found in drier fields and pastures, while Snowy Egrets prefer swamps and open water.

## Illustrations

Illustrations show the adult bird in the plumage most likely to be encountered during the season(s) it is in Colorado. If it is likely that you will see more than one type of plumage during this time, the alternate plumage is shown as well. For birds that are sexually dimorphic (females and males look different), I have usually included illustrations of both sexes. Other plumages, such as those of juveniles and alternate morphs, are described in the text.

# Bird Topography and Terms

Bird topography describes the outer surface of a bird and how its various anatomical structures fit together. Below is a diagram outlining the terms most commonly used to describe the feathers and bare parts of a bird.

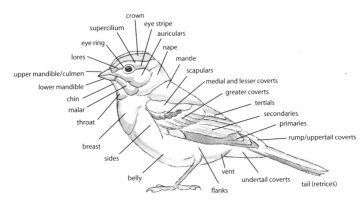

# NONPASSERINES

**Canada Goose,** *Branta canadensis*
Family Anatidae (Geese, Ducks, Mergansers)
**Size:** 27–35", depending on race
**Season:** Winter; during spring and fall migrations
**Habitat:** Marshes, grasslands, public parks,
golf courses

1/27/15

The Canada Goose is the state's most common goose, and is found in suburban settings. It is vegetarian, foraging on land for grass, seeds, and grain or in the water by upending like the dabbling ducks. It has a heavy body with short, thick legs and a long neck. Overall, its coloring is barred gray-brown with a white rear, short black tail, black neck, and a white patch running under the neck to behind the eye. During its powerful flight the white rump makes a semicircular patch between the tail and back. Voice is a loud honk. In flight Canada geese form the classic *V* formation. (Illustration shows an adult.)

**Snow Goose,** *Chen caerulescens*
Family Anatidae (Geese, Ducks,
Mergansers)
**Size:** 28"
**Season:** Spring and fall during migration
**Habitat:** Grasslands, marshes

The Snow Goose forms huge, impressive flocks when it visits Colorado during spring and fall migrations between the arctic tundra and southern North America and Mexico. It has two color forms: the "blue" and more common "white." The white form is predominantly white, with black outer wing feathers and a pale yellowish wash to the face during summer. The blue form retains the white head and lower belly but is otherwise dark slate gray or brownish gray. In both morphs, its bill is thick at the base, pink, and has a black patch where the mandibles meet. Legs of both types are pink. Snow Geese feed mostly on the ground, consuming shoots, roots, grains, and insects. The similar Ross's Goose is smaller, with a shorter bill. (Illustration shows a white morph adult.)

## Wood Duck, *Aix sponsa*
Family Anatidae (Geese, Ducks, Mergansers)
**Size:** 18″
**Season:** Summer in northeastern Colorado
**Habitat:** Wooded ponds, swamps

The regal Wood Duck is among the dabbling ducks, or those that tip headfirst into shallow water to pluck aquatic plants and animals from the bottom. The male is long-tailed and small-billed, with a dark back, light buff-colored flanks, and sharp black-and-white head patterning. He also sports a bushy head crest that droops behind the nape. The female is gray-brown with spotting along the undersides and a conspicuous white teardrop-shaped eye patch. Both sexes swim with their heads angled downward as if in a nod, and they have sharp claws, which they use to cling to branches and snags. (Illustration shows a breeding male, below, and a female, above.)

## Mallard, *Anas platyrhynchos*
Family Anatidae (Geese, Ducks, Mergansers)
**Size:** 23″
**Season:** Year-round
**Habitat:** Parks, urban areas, virtually any water environment

The ubiquitous Mallard is the most abundant duck in the Northern Hemisphere. It is a classic dabbling duck, plunging its head into the water with its tail up, searching for aquatic plants, animals, and snails. It will also eat worms, seeds, insects, and even mice. Noisy and quacking, it is heavy but a strong flier. The male has a dark head with green or blue iridescence, a white neck ring, and a large yellow bill. The underparts are pale with a chestnut brown breast. The female is plain brownish with buff-colored, scalloped markings. She also has a dark eye line and an orangey bill with a dark center. The speculum is blue on both sexes, and the tail coverts often curl upward. Mallards form huge floating flocks called "rafts." To achieve flight, it lifts straight into the air without running. (Illustration shows a breeding male, below, and a female, above.)

### Gadwall, *Anas strepera*
Family Anatidae (Geese, Ducks, Mergansers)
**Size:** 20½"
**Season:** Year-round in eastern Colorado
**Habitat:** Shallow lakes, marshes

The Gadwall is a buoyant, plain-colored dabbling duck with a steep forehead and a somewhat angular head. The breeding male is grayish overall, with very fine variegation and barring. The rump and undertail coverts are black, the scapulars are light orange-brown, the tertials are gray, and the head is lighter below the eye and darker above. Females and nonbreeding males are mottled brown with few distinguishing markings. In flight there is a distinctive white speculum that is most prominent in males. Gadwalls dabble or dive for a variety of aquatic plants and invertebrates, and often gather in large flocks away from the shore. (Illustration shows a breeding male, below, and a female, above.)

### American Widgeon, *Anas americana*

Family Anatidae (Geese, Ducks, Mergansers)
**Size:** 19"
**Season:** Winter; spring and fall migrations
**Habitat:** Shallow ponds, fields

The American Widgeon is also known as the Baldpate, in reference to its white crown. A wary and easily alarmed duck, it feeds from the water's surface, often gleaning prey stirred up by the efforts of diving ducks. The underside is a light cinnamon color with white undertail coverts, and the back is light brown. The male has a white crown and forehead with a very slight crest when seen in profile. A glossy dark green patch extends from the eye to the back of the neck. A white wing covert patch can usually be seen on the folded wing, but is more obvious in flight. The head of the female is unmarked and brownish. (Illustration shows a breeding male, below, and a female, above.)

**Northern Pintail,** *Anas acuta*
Family Anatidae (Geese, Ducks, Mergansers)
**Size:** 21"
**Season:** Year-round
**Habitat:** Marshes, shallow lakes

Among the most abundant ducks in North America, the Northern Pintail is an elegant, slender, dabbling duck with a long neck, small head, and narrow wings. In breeding plumage the male has long, pointed central tail feathers. It is gray along its back and sides, with a brown head and a white breast. A white stripe extends from the breast along the back of the neck. The female is mottled brown and tan overall, with a light brown head. To feed, the Northern Pintail bobs its head into the water to capture aquatic invertebrates and plants from the muddy bottom. It rises directly out of the water to take flight. (Illustration shows a breeding male, below, and a female, above.)

**Northern Shoveler,**
*Anas clypeata*
Family Anatidae (Geese, Ducks, Mergansers)
**Size:** 19"
**Season:** Summer
**Habitat:** Shallow marshes, lakes, bays

Also known as the Spoonbill Duck, the Northern Shoveler skims the surface of the water with its neck extended, scooping up aquatic animals and plants with its long, spatula-like bill. It also sucks up ooze from the muddy bottoms of its habitats and strains it through bristles at the edge of its bill, retaining worms, leeches, and snails. This medium-size duck seems top-heavy due to its large bill. Plumage in the male is white on the underside, with a large, chestnut-colored side patch, a dark green head, and a gray bill. The female is pale brown overall, with an orangey bill. (Illustration shows a breeding male, below, and a female, above.)

### Cinnamon Teal, *Anas cyanoptera*
Family Anatidae (Geese, Ducks, Mergansers)
**Size:** 16″
**Season:** Summer
**Habitat:** Marshes, shallow lakes

The Cinnamon Teal is a small dabbling duck with a wide, spatulate bill. The breeding male is cinnamon brown overall, with darker hindquarters and paler, sharply shaped back feathers. The eye is golden red and the bill is dark gray. Females and nonbreeding males are a paler shade of cinnamon with scalloped plumage, and closely resemble the Blue-winged Teal. In flight, note the blue inner wing patch and the white underwing. Cinnamon Teals dabble in shallow water for plant material, insects, and aquatic invertebrates, filtering mud through their wide bills. (Illustration shows a breeding male, below, and a female, above.)

### Blue-winged Teal, *Anas discors*
Family Anatidae (Geese, Ducks, Mergansers)
**Size:** 16″
**Season:** Summer
**Habitat:** Freshwater marshes, mudflats, wet agricultural areas

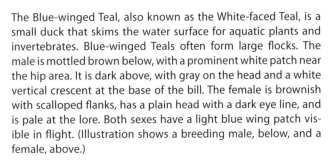

The Blue-winged Teal, also known as the White-faced Teal, is a small duck that skims the water surface for aquatic plants and invertebrates. Blue-winged Teals often form large flocks. The male is mottled brown below, with a prominent white patch near the hip area. It is dark above, with gray on the head and a white vertical crescent at the base of the bill. The female is brownish with scalloped flanks, has a plain head with a dark eye line, and is pale at the lore. Both sexes have a light blue wing patch visible in flight. (Illustration shows a breeding male, below, and a female, above.)

### Green-winged Teal, *Anas crecca*
Family Anatidae (Geese, Ducks, Mergansers)
**Size:** 14"
**Season:** Year-round in northern Colorado; winter elsewhere in the state
**Habitat:** Marshes, ponds

The Green-winged Teal is a cute, very small, active duck with a small, thin bill. The breeding male is silvery gray with a dotted, tawny breast patch, a pale yellow hip patch, and a distinct, vertical white bar on its side. The head is rusty brown with an iridescent green patch around and behind the eye. Females and nonbreeding males are mottled brown with a dark eye line and white belly. Green-winged Teals dabble in the shallows for plant material and small invertebrates. They are quick and agile in flight, and sport a bright green speculum. They form very large winter flocks. (Illustration shows a breeding male, below, and a female, above.)

### Canvasback, *Aythya valisineria*
Family Anatidae (Geese, Ducks, Mergansers)
**Size:** 21"
**Season:** Transient spring and fall migrant
**Habitat:** Grassy wetlands, lakes

The Canvasback is a stocky, thick-necked diving duck with a long, shallow forehead that slopes into the angle of the bill. The middle section of the breeding male, including back, wings, and belly, is entirely white. The tail and breast are black, and the head is a rusty brown that is darker on the crown and front of the face. The eye is deep red. Females are very pale overall, with a light, canvas-colored back and a tan head and neck. The Canvasback runs across the water to take flight, whereupon the light middle and darker ends are striking. It usually feeds by diving for aquatic plants. (Illustration shows a breeding male.)

### Redhead, *Aythya americana*
Family Anatidae (Geese, Ducks, Mergansers)
**Size:** 19"
**Season:** Year-round
**Habitat:** Shallow lakes, marshes

The Redhead is a heavy-bodied diving duck with a steep forehead and a large, rounded head. The breeding male is pale gray with a dark rear end and breast. The head is light rusty brown, the eye is yellow, and the bill is bluish with a black tip. The female is brownish gray overall, with pale areas at the base of the bill and throat. The upper side of the wing has white flight feathers and dark gray coverts. These birds "run" across the water to become airborne. They forage by diving for aquatic plants and invertebrates, and may form huge, floating "rafts" during the winter. Redheads are similar in pattern to the larger Canvasbacks. (Illustration shows a breeding male, below, and a female, above.)

### Ring-necked Duck, *Aythya collaris*
Family Anatidae (Geese, Ducks, Mergansers)
**Size:** 17"
**Season:** Spring and fall during migration
**Habitat:** Shallow lakes and ponds near woodlands

The Ring-necked Duck, also known as the Ring-billed Duck, is classified as a diving duck, typically swimming underwater to find plant and animal prey, although it may also behave like a dabbling duck and bob for food at the surface. This small, gregarious duck looks tall, with a postlike head and neck and a peaked crown. The breeding male is stunning, with contrasting light and dark plumage and a dark, metallic brown-purple head. The base of its bill is edged with white feathers, and the bill itself is gray with a white ring and black tip. The ring around the neck, for which the duck is named, is actually a very inconspicuous brownish band at the bottom of the neck in the male bird. The female is brownish overall, with a white eye ring. (Illustration shows a breeding male, below, and a female, above.)

### Lesser Scaup, *Aythya affinis*
Family Anatidae (Geese, Ducks, Mergansers)
**Size:** 17"
**Season:** Spring and fall during migration
**Habitat:** Marshes, shallow lakes

The Lesser Scaup is a small, short-bodied duck with a tall head profile and a relatively thin bill. The breeding male is distinctly two-toned, with white sides, a pale, variegated gray back, and a black rear end and front. The head has a dark, metallic violet or greenish cast in good light, and the bill has a small black dot at the nail. The nonbreeding male is paler, with brown on its sides. Females are gray-brown with a dark brown head and a white patch at the base of the bill. This diving duck forages for aquatic plants and insects. It is very similar to the Greater Scaup, but is smaller and has a more peaked head. (Illustration shows a breeding male, below, and a female, above.)

### Common Goldeneye,
*Bucephala clangula*
Family Anatidae (Geese, Ducks, Mergansers)
**Size:** 18½"
**Season:** Winter
**Habitat:** Lakes, rivers

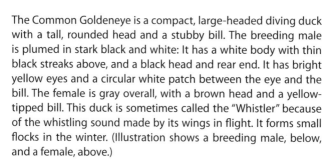

The Common Goldeneye is a compact, large-headed diving duck with a tall, rounded head and a stubby bill. The breeding male is plumed in stark black and white: It has a white body with thin black streaks above, and a black head and rear end. It has bright yellow eyes and a circular white patch between the eye and the bill. The female is gray overall, with a brown head and a yellow-tipped bill. This duck is sometimes called the "Whistler" because of the whistling sound made by its wings in flight. It forms small flocks in the winter. (Illustration shows a breeding male, below, and a female, above.)

### Bufflehead, *Bucephala albeola*
Family Anatidae (Geese, Ducks, Mergansers)
**Size:** 14"
**Season:** Winter
**Habitat:** Lakes, rivers

The Bufflehead is a diminutive diving duck—indeed, the smallest duck in North America. Also known as the Bumblebee Duck, it forms small flocks that forage in open water for aquatic plants and invertebrates. The duck's puffy, rounded head seems large for its body and small, gray-blue bill. The breeding male is striking, with a large white patch on the back half of its head that contrasts with the black front of the head and its black back. The male's underside is white. The female is paler overall, with a dark gray-brown head and an airfoil-shaped white patch behind the eye. Flight is low to the water with rapid wing beats. (Illustration shows a breeding male, below, and a female, above.)

### Common Merganser,
*Mergus merganser*
Family Anatidae (Geese, Ducks, Mergansers)
**Size:** 25"
**Season:** Year-round but best in winter
**Habitat:** Lakes, rivers

The Common Merganser is a long, sleek, diving duck with a rounded head and long, thin bill. The breeding male is dark gray above and white (sometimes washed with pale brown) below. The head is black with a metallic green sheen, and the bill is red with a dark tip. The female looks similar to the nonbreeding male, gray overall with a rusty brown head and a white chin and neck. Also known as the Sawtooth, the Common Merganser dives for fish or aquatic invertebrates and grips its prey with the sawlike serrations on its bill. It runs across the water to take off, but flight is fast and direct. (Illustration shows a breeding male, below, and a female, above.)

## Red-breasted Merganser, *Mergus serrator*
Family Anatidae (Geese, Ducks, Mergansers)
**Size:** 23"
**Season:** Spring and fall during migration
**Habitat:** Lakes near woodlands, rivers

The mergansers are known as the Fishing Ducks or Sawtooths. They dive and chase fish of considerable size underwater and secure their catches with long, thin bills that are serrated along the edges. Both male and female Red-breasted Mergansers sport a fine, long, two-part crest. The male has a white band around its neck, a dark head, red bill, and gray flanks. The female is grayish overall, with a brown head. The nonbreeding male closely resembles the female. Flight is low and quick on pointed wings. (Illustration shows a breeding male, below, and a female, above.)

## Ruddy Duck, *Oxyura jamaicencis*
Family Anatidae (Geese, Ducks, Mergansers)
**Size:** 15"
**Season:** Summer
**Habitat:** Open water, wetlands

The Ruddy Duck is a "stiff-tailed duck," part of a group known for rigid tail feathers that are often cocked up in display. It dives deep for its food, which consists of aquatic vegetation, and flies low over the water with quick wing beats. A relatively small duck with a big head and a flat, broad body, the breeding male is a rich sienna brown overall, with white cheeks, a black cap and nape, and a bright blue bill. The female is drab with a conspicuous dark stripe across the cheek. Nonbreeding males become gray. The Ruddy Duck can sink low into the water, grebelike, and will often dive to escape danger. (Illustration shows a breeding male, below, and a female, above.)

### Ring-necked Pheasant, *Phasianus colchicus*
Family Phasianidae (Pheasants, Grouse, Turkeys)
**Size:** Male to 21", female to 34"
**Season:** Year-round
**Habitat:** Grasslands, woodland edges, agricultural land with brushy cover

The Ring-necked Pheasant is a large, chicken-shaped bird with a long, pointed tail. The male is ornately patterned in rufous tones, gold, and blue-gray, with pale spotting on the wings and back and dark spotting underneath. The head is an iridescent green-blue with red facial skin and a tufted crown. There is a white ring about the neck. The female is mottled brown above and plain below, without obvious head markings. They peck on the ground for seeds, grasses, and insects. Vocalizations include a harsh *Auk caw* and muffled wing fluttering. (Illustration shows an adult male.)

### Dusky Grouse,
*Dendragapus obscurus*
Family Phasianidae (Pheasants, Grouse, Turkeys)
**Size:** 19"; male larger than female
**Season:** Year-round
**Habitat:** Forest edges, open brushland, mountain ridges

The Dusky Grouse of the interior was once considered a Blue Grouse, the same species as the Pacific region's Sooty Grouse. It is a large, heavy grouse with a long tail and thick, feathered legs. The male is finely marked gray-brown overall, with some white patterning along the back, wings, and sides. It has a relatively thick bill and an orange-red comb above the eye. In display it spreads its neck feathers to reveal a circle of white feathers around a bare patch of reddish skin. The female is extensively mottled gray, brown, and white overall. The Dusky Grouse forages on the ground for seeds, berries, and insects, and voices a deep, soft, resonant *Yoop, yoop.* Strangely, they move from low elevations in summer to higher elevations in the winter. (Illustration shows an adult male.)

## White-tailed Ptarmigan, *Lagopus leucura*
Family Phasianidae (Pheasants, Grouse, Turkeys)
**Size:** 13"; male larger than female
**Season:** Year-round
**Habitat:** High elevations in treeless, mountainous areas; tundra zones

The White-tailed Ptarmigan is a small, chunky, grouselike bird with a small head and bill. The breeding male is white below with dark spotting on the breast and sides, and mottled brown above and on the central tail area. Above the eye is a red comb. Nonbreeding adults of both sexes are all white except for black eyes and bills. The breeding female is mottled brown overall, but has white wings and corners of the tail. Legs and toes are feathered for arctic conditions. White-tailed Ptarmigans forage on the ground for plant buds, insects, and berries. (Illustration shows a breeding male, below, and a nonbreeding male, above.)

## Greater Sage-Grouse, *Centrocerus urophasianus*
Family Phasianidae (Pheasants, Grouse, Turkeys)
**Size:** 28"; male larger than female
**Season:** Year-round
**Habitat:** Open sagebrush country

The Greater Sage-Grouse is Colorado's largest grouse. It is a heavy bird with a relatively small head and a long, pointed tail. The male is well camouflaged: mottled gray-brown on the back with a clean, white breast and a black belly. The head has a black throat and white streaking along the neck, and there is a sage green comb above the eyes. The female is mottled gray-brown overall, with a plainer head, but it retains the black belly. The male engages in a dramatic display posture during courtship, with its tail spread and raised and its breast feathers spread to reveal two yellow air sacs. The air sacs produce a low "gloop" or hooting noise. The grouse feed almost exclusively on sagebrush. (Illustration shows an adult male.)

**Wild Turkey,** *Meleagris gallopavo*
Family Phasianidae (Pheasants, Grouse, Turkeys)
**Size:** 36–48"; male larger than female
**Season:** Year-round
**Habitat:** Open mixed woodlands

The Wild Turkey is a very large, dark, ground-dwelling bird (but slimmer than the domestic variety). The head and neck appear small for the body size, and the legs are thick and stout. The heavily barred plumage is quite iridescent in strong light. The head and neck are covered with bluish, warty, crinkled bare skin that droops under the chin in a red wattle. Often foraging in flocks, they roam the ground for seeds, grubs, and insects, then roost at night in trees. Males emit the familiar *Gobble*, while females are less vocal, making a soft clucking sound. In display the male hunches up with its tail up and spread like a giant fan. Southwestern races, which are seen in Colorado, show white banding on the tail. (Illustration shows an adult male.)

**Pied-billed Grebe**, *Podilymbus podiceps*
Family Podicipedidae (Grebes)
**Size:** 13"
**Season:** Year-round in southern Colorado; summer in northern Colorado
**Habitat:** Freshwater ponds and lakes

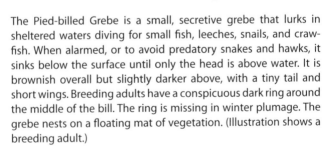

The Pied-billed Grebe is a small, secretive grebe that lurks in sheltered waters diving for small fish, leeches, snails, and crawfish. When alarmed, or to avoid predatory snakes and hawks, it sinks below the surface until only the head is above water. It is brownish overall but slightly darker above, with a tiny tail and short wings. Breeding adults have a conspicuous dark ring around the middle of the bill. The ring is missing in winter plumage. The grebe nests on a floating mat of vegetation. (Illustration shows a breeding adult.)

### Eared Grebe, *Podiceps nigricollis*
Family Podicipedidae (Grebes)
**Size:** 13"
**Season:** Summer
**Habitat:** Shallow freshwater ponds and lakes

The Eared Grebe is a small, thin grebe with a narrow, pointed bill that turns up at the tip. The breeding adult has a black head, neck, and back, a pale belly, and rufous sides. The head has a peaked crown, bright red eyes, and golden yellow ear tufts. In winter the birds have whitish head markings, breasts, and sides, with no ear tufts. Note the clean, white secondary patch that can be seen on the wing in flight. The tail is tiny and hidden. Eared Grebes are gregarious, forming large nesting colonies, and forage by diving for aquatic invertebrates and insects. They are slightly more buoyant than other grebes. (Illustration shows a breeding adult.)

### Western Grebe,
*Aechmorphorus occidentalis*
Family Podicipedidae (Grebes)
**Size:** 25"
**Season:** Summer
**Habitat:** Shallow lakes, marshes

The Western Grebe is a large, elegant grebe with an extremely long, thin neck and a long, pointed, greenish yellow bill with an upturned lower mandible. It is slate gray above and crisp white below. The head and neck are cleanly divided in black and white, with black encompassing the red eye (unlike the similar Clark's Grebe). Western Grebes dive for fish and aquatic invertebrates, and voice a high-pitched, rattling *Kreek-Kreek*. They rarely take flight, but do so following a long, labored run across the water surface. It was once considered the same species as the Clark's Grebe. (Illustration shows a breeding adult.)

## Double-crested Cormorant,
*Phalacrocorax auritus*
Family Phalacrocoracidae (Cormorants)
**Size:** 32"
**Season:** Summer; during spring and fall migrations
**Habitat:** Open water

Named for the two long, white plumes that emerge from behind the eyes during breeding season, the Double-crested Cormorant is an expert swimmer that dives underwater to chase down fish. Because its plumage lacks the normal oils to repel water, it will stand with wings outstretched to dry itself. These cormorants are solid black with a pale glossy cast on the back and wings. The eye is bright green, the bill is thin and hooked, and the throat patch and lores are yellow. (Illustration shows a breeding adult.)

## American White Pelican,
*Pelecanus erythrorhynchos*
Family Pelecanidae (Pelicans)
**Size:** 62"
**Season:** Spring and fall migrations
**Habitat:** Open freshwater

One of North America's largest birds, the American White Pelican has a wingspan of over 9 feet. It is white overall, with black flight feathers. The massive bill is orange with a membranous, expandable throat pouch. In posture it holds its neck in a characteristic strong kink and its folded wings in a peak along the back. The pelican often feeds in cooperative groups, herding fish as they swim and scooping them up by dipping their bills in the water. The White Pelican never plunge-dives like the Brown Pelican. When breeding, a strange horny growth appears on the upper mandible in both sexes. (Illustration shows a non-breeding adult.)

### American Bittern,
*Botaurus lentiginosus*
Family Ardeidae (Herons, Egrets)
**Size:** 27"
**Season:** Summer
**Habitat:** Marshy areas with dense vegetation

The American Bittern is a fairly large, secretive heron with a small head, a long, straight bill, and a thick body. It has a habit of standing still with its neck and bill pointed straight up to imitate the surrounding reeds. Its plumage is very cryptic: Above, it is variegated brown and tan, and below it is pale brown or whitish with thick, rust-colored streaking that extends up the neck. The bill is yellow-green and dark on the upper mandible. A dark patch extends from the lower bill to the upper neck. The legs are yellow-green and thick. American Bitterns skulk slowly through reeds and grasses to catch frogs, insects, and invertebrates. (Illustration shows an adult.)

### Great Blue Heron,
*Ardea herodias*
Family Ardeidae (Herons, Egrets)
**Size:** 46"
**Season:** Year-round
**Habitat:** Most aquatic areas, including lakes, creeks, and marshes

The Great Blue Heron is the largest heron in North America. Walking slowly through shallow water or fields, it stalks fish, crabs, and small vertebrates, catching them with its massive bill. With long legs and a long neck, the heron is blue-gray overall, with a white face and a heavy yellow-orange bill. The crown is black, and supports plumes of medium length. The front of the neck is white, with distinct black chevrons fading into breast plumes. In flight the neck is tucked back and the wing beats are regular and labored. (Illustration shows an adult.)

**Snowy Egret**, *Egretta thula*
Family Ardeidae (Herons, Egrets)
**Size:** 24"
**Season:** Summer
**Habitat:** Open water, marshes, swamps

The Snowy Egret is all white, with lacy plumes across the back in breeding season. The bill is slim and black, and the legs are black with bright yellow feet. The juvenile has greenish legs with a yellow stripe along the front. The egret forages for fish and frogs along shorelines by moving quickly, shuffling to stir up prey, and stabbing the prey with its bill. Sometimes it may run to pursue its quarry. You can remember the name of this bird by keeping in mind that it wears yellow "boots" because it is cold, or "snowy." (Illustration shows a breeding adult.)

HERONS, EGRETS

**Cattle Egret,** *Bubulcus ibis*
Family Ardeidae (Herons, Egrets)
**Size:** 20"
**Season:** Summer in eastern Colorado
**Habitat:** Upland fields, often near cattle in grazing land

The Cattle Egret is a widespread species, originally from Africa and now quite common in the southeastern United States. Unlike most herons, it is not normally found in aquatic environments. It forms groups around cattle, often perching atop them, and feeds on insects aroused by the movement of their hooves. It is stocky, all white, and has a comparatively short, yellow bill and short, black legs. In breeding plumage the legs and bill turn a bright orange, and a peachy, pale yellow color forms on the crown, breast, and back. (Illustration shows a nonbreeding adult.)

### Green Heron, *Butorides virensens*
Family Ardeidae (Herons, Egrets)
**Size:** 18"
**Season:** Summer in southeastern Colorado
**Habitat:** Ponds, creeks, wetlands

The Green Heron is a compact, crow-size bird that perches on low branches over the water, crouching forward to search for fish, snails, and insects. It is known to toss a bug into the water to attract fish. The Green Heron is really not so green, but a dull grayish blue with a burgundy/chestnut-colored neck and a black crown. The bill is dark and the legs are bright yellow-orange. When disturbed, its crest feathers will stand up, and the heron will stand erect and twitch its tail. The species is fairly secretive and solitary. (Illustration shows an adult.)

### Black-crowned Night-Heron,
*Nycticorax nycticorax*
Family Ardeidae (Herons, Egrets)
**Size:** 25"
**Season:** Summer
**Habitat:** Marshes, swamps with wooded banks

The nocturnal Black-crowned Night-Heron is a stocky, thick-necked heron with a comparatively large head and a sharp, heavy, thick bill. It has pale gray wings, white underparts, and a black crown, back, and bill. The eyes are piercing red and the legs are yellow. In breeding plumage it develops long, white plumes on the rear of its head. During the day the herons roost in groups, but at night they forage alone, waiting motionless for prey such as fish or crabs. They may even raid the nests of other birds. The heron's voice is composed of low-pitched barks and croaks. (Illustration shows an adult.)

### White-faced Ibis, *Plegadis chihi*
Family Threskiornithidae (Ibises)
**Size:** 23"
**Season:** Summer
**Habitat:** Swamps, fields, shallows in freshwater lakes

The White-faced Ibis is somewhat heronlike in shape, with a relatively short neck and a long, down-curved, grayish bill. The plumage is dark, metallic green-black on the wings and back, with a dark chestnut body, neck, and head. The lores are reddish and bordered with white feathers that encircle the dark red eye. In winter, adults of both sexes are dark overall, with pale streaking on the head and neck, and they lack white feathers around the eyes. Breeding adults have bright red legs. Unlike herons, ibises fly with their necks extended. They walk steadily while picking and probing with long bills for aquatic invertebrates, and they roost in trees. (Illustration shows a breeding adult.)

### Turkey Vulture, *Cathartes aura*
Family Cathartidae (New World Vultures)
**Size:** 27"
**Season:** Summer
**Habitat:** Open, dry country

The Turkey Vulture is known for its effortless, skilled soaring. It will often soar for hours, without flapping, rocking in the breeze on 6-foot wings that form an upright V shape, or dihedral angle. It has a black body and inner wing, with pale flight feathers and pale tail feathers that give it a noticeable two-toned appearance from below. The tail is longish, and the feet extend no more than halfway past the base of the tail. The head is naked, red, and small, so the bird appears almost headless in flight. The bill is strongly hooked to aid in tearing apart its favored food—carrion. Juveniles have a dark gray head. Turkey Vultures often roost in flocks and form groups around food or at a roadkill site. (Illustration shows an adult.)

### Osprey, *Pandion haliaetus*
Family Pandionidae (Osprey)
**Size:** 23"; female larger than male
**Season:** Summer; spring and fall migrant
**Habitat:** Always near water, salt or fresh

Also known as the Fish Hawk, the Osprey exhibits a dramatic feeding method: It plunges feet first into the water to snag fish. Sometimes it completely submerges itself, then laboriously flies off with its heavy catch. It is dark brown above, white below, and has a distinct dark eye stripe contiguous with the nape. Females show a dark, mottled "necklace" across their breasts, and juveniles have pale streaking on their backs. Ospreys fly with an obvious crook at the wrist, appearing gull-like. Wings are long and narrow, with a dark carpal patch. (Illustration shows an adult.)

### Northern Harrier, *Circus cyaneus*
Family Accipitridae (Hawks, Eagles)
**Size:** 18"; female larger than male
**Season:** Year-round
**Habitat:** Open fields, wetlands

Also known as the Marsh Hawk, the Northern Harrier flies low to the ground, methodically surveying its hunting grounds for rodents and other small animals. When it spots prey, aided by its acute hearing, it will drop abruptly to the ground to attack. It is a thin raptor with a long tail and long, flame-shaped wings that are broad in the middle. The face has a distinct owl-like facial disk, and there is a conspicuous white patch at the rump. Males are gray above, with a white, streaked breast and black wing tips. Females are brown with a barred breast. The juvenile is similar in plumage to the female, but with a pale belly. (Illustration shows a female, below, and a male, above.)

### Sharp-shinned Hawk,
*Accipiter striatus*
Family Accipitridae (Hawks, Eagles)
**Size:** 10–14"; female larger than male
**Season:** Year-round
**Habitat:** Woodlands, bushy areas

The Sharp-shinned Hawk is Colorado's smallest accipiter, with a longish, squared tail and stubby, rounded wings. Its short wings allow for agile flight in tight, wooded quarters, where it quickly attacks small birds in flight. It is grayish above and light below, barred with pale rufous stripes. The eyes are set forward on the face to aid in the direct pursuit of prey. The juvenile is white below, streaked with brown. The Sharp-shinned Hawk may be confused with the larger Cooper's Hawk. (Illustration shows an adult.)

### Cooper's Hawk, *Accipiter cooperii*
Family Accipitridae (Hawks, Eagles)
**Size:** 17"; female larger than male
**Season:** Year-round
**Habitat:** Woodlands

The Cooper's Hawk perches stealthily on branches in the canopy, then ambushes its prey of smaller birds or mammals by diving through thickets. Its plumage is very similar to that of the Sharp-shinned Hawk, although it is larger in size, has a slightly longer, rounded tail and thinner wings, and sports a relatively larger head. The eyes are set in the middle of the face. Unlike Sharp-shinned Hawks, Cooper's Hawks may perch and hunt in open country. (Illustration shows an adult.)

### Northern Goshawk, *Accipiter gentilis*
Family Accipitridae (Hawks, Eagles)
**Size:** 22"; female larger than male
**Season:** Year-round
**Habitat:** Mountains, forests

The Northern Goshawk is Colorado's largest accipiter, similar in shape to the Cooper's and Sharp-shinned Hawks, but often mistaken for a buteo because of its large size. It is dark gray on the back and finely barred white and gray underneath. The head has a white superciliary stripe bordered by a dark crown and ear patch. Juveniles are mottled brown with coarse streaking across the breast, and have more noticeably banded tails. Northern Goshawks hunt from a perch, ambush-style, flying through woodlands to capture birds and mammals up to rabbit size. (Illustration shows an adult.)

### Swainson's Hawk,
*Buteo swainsoni*
Family Accipitridae (Hawks, Eagles)
**Size:** 19"; female larger than male
**Season:** Summer
**Habitat:** Dry prairies, open fields

The Swainson's Hawk is a buteo with a long tail, long wings with pointed tips, and a relatively small, rounded head. It has variable plumage colors, ranging from dark morphs to the more common light morphs. The light morph has a white underside, a dark brown back, a rufous breast, and white lores and chin. Darker forms become rufous or dark brown on the breast and belly. In flight the light morph has pale wing linings and a pale belly that contrasts with its darker flight feathers and tail. Swainson's Hawks feed on small mammals, insects, and reptiles, either descending from a perch or by stalking on the ground. The hawk's voice is a high-pitched *Eeeeww*. (Illustration shows a light morph adult.)

### Red-tailed Hawk,
*Buteo jamaicensis*
Family Accipitridae (Hawks, Eagles)
**Size:** 20"
**Season:** Year-round
**Habitat:** Prairies, open country

This widespread species is the most common buteo in the United States. It has broad, rounded wings and a stout hooked bill. Its plumage is highly variable depending on geographic location. In general the underparts are light, with darker streaking that forms a dark band across the belly, the upperparts are dark brown, and the tail is rufous. Light spotting occurs along the scapulars. In flight there is a noticeable dark patch along the inner leading edge of the underwing. Red-tailed Hawks glide down from perches, such as telephone poles and posts in open country, to catch rodents. They also may hover to spot prey. They are usually seen alone or in pairs. The voice is the familiar *Keeer!* (Illustration shows a western adult.)

### Ferruginous Hawk, *Buteo regalis*
Family Accipitridae (Hawks, Eagles)
**Size:** 23"; female larger than male
**Season:** Year-round
**Habitat:** Dry prairies, open country

The Ferruginous Hawk is Colorado's largest buteo. It has a thick body and neck, a large, hooked bill, and long, broad wings. Two color morphs occur: light and dark. The light morph is white below with rufous barring on the flanks and thighs. The back is mottled brown and rufous, with grayish flight feathers. The dark morph is dark brown overall, with white on the undersides of the flight feathers and tail. Ferruginous Hawks stalk their prey of small mammals from a perch, or by hovering or soaring. (Illustration shows a light morph adult.)

### Golden Eagle, *Aquila chrysaetos*
Family Accipitridae (Hawks, Eagles)
**Size:** 30"; female larger than male
**Season:** Year-round
**Habitat:** Mountainous areas, hills,
open country

The Golden Eagle is a solitary, very large, buteo-shaped raptor with large talons and long, broad wings, with a 6½-foot wingspan. Its plumage is dark brown overall, with a pale golden nape and a relatively small head. The bill is large and hooked, and forms a wide gape. The juvenile shows a white patch at the base of the tail and at the base of the flight feathers. Golden Eagles hold their wings horizontal or with a very slight dihedral angle in flight. They forage from a perch or by soaring overhead, attacking mammals, reptiles, and birds. They may also eat carrion. (Illustration shows an adult.)

### Bald Eagle,
*Haliaeetus leucocephalus*
Family Accipitridae (Hawks, Eagles)
**Size:** 30–40"; female larger than male
**Season:** Year-round or during winter
**Habitat:** Lakes, rivers with tall perches
or cliffs

The Bald Eagle is a large raptor that is fairly uncommon even though its range is widespread. It eats fish or scavenges dead animals, and congregates in large numbers where food is abundant. Plumage is dark brown, which contrasts with its white head and tail. Juveniles show white splotching across the wings and breast. The yellow bill is large and powerful, and the talons are large and sharp. In flight the Bald Eagle holds its wings fairly flat and straight, resembling a long plank. Bald Eagles make huge nests of sticks high in trees. (Illustration shows an adult.)

### American Kestrel,
*Falco sparverius*
Family Falconidae (Falcons)
**Size:** 10"
**Season:** Year-round
**Habitat:** Open country,
urban areas

Colorado's most common falcon, the American Kestrel is a tiny, robin-size falcon with long, pointed wings and tail, and fast flight. It hovers above fields or dives from a perch in branches or on a wire to capture small animals and insects. The kestrel's upperparts are rufous and barred with black, its wings are blue-gray, and its breast is buff colored or white and streaked with black spots. The head is patterned with a gray crown and vertical patches of black down the face. The female has rufous wings and a barred tail. Also known as the Sparrow Hawk, the kestrel has a habit of flicking its tail up and down while perched. (Illustration shows an adult male.)

### Prairie Falcon, *Falco mexicanus*
Family Falconidae (Falcons)
**Size:** 17"; female larger than male
**Season:** Year-round
**Habitat:** Prairies, open land near cliffs
and mountains

The Prairie Falcon is large, with a long tail and narrow, pointed wings. The body is pale brown-gray above, and white below with brown streaking. The head is patterned with a white ear patch and chin, a dark malar patch, and a large, black eye. The underside in flight is marked with dark inner wing coverts and axillar (armpit) feathers. Prairie Falcons attack small animals on the ground from a perch or after aerial pursuit. (Illustration shows an adult.)

## Peregrine Falcon,
*Falco peregrinus*
Family Falconidae (Falcons)
**Size:** 17"; female larger than male
**Season:** Summer
**Habitat:** Open country, cliffs, urban areas

The Peregrine Falcon is a powerful and agile raptor with long, sharply pointed wings. It is dark, slate gray above and pale whitish below, with uniform barring below the breast. Plumage on the head forms a distinctive "helmet," with a white ear patch and chin contrasting with the blackish face and crown. Juveniles are mottled brown overall, with heavy streaking on the underside. Peregrine Falcons attack other birds in flight using spectacular high-speed aerial dives. Once threatened by DDT pollution that caused thinning of their eggshells, the Peregrine Falcon has made a dramatic comeback. (Illustration shows an adult.)

## American Coot, *Fulica americana*
Family Rallidae (Rails, Coots)
**Size:** 15"
**Season:** Year-round
**Habitat:** Wetlands, ponds, urban lawns, parks

The American Coot has a plump body and a thick head and neck. It is very common and becomes relatively tame in urban areas and parks. To feed, the coot dives for fish, but it will also dabble like a duck or pick food from the ground. The American Coot is dark gray overall, with a black head and white bill that ends with a dark narrow ring. The white trailing edge of the wings can be seen in flight. The toes are flanked with lobes that enable the coot to walk on water plants and swim efficiently. Juveniles are similar in plumage to adults, but are paler. Coots are often seen in very large flocks. (Illustration shows an adult.)

**Sora,** *Porzana carolina*
Family Rallidae (Rails, Coots)
**Size:** 9″
**Season:** Summer
**Habitat:** Marshes, meadows

The Sora is a small, short-tailed, chicken-shaped rail with long, thin toes. Its plumage is mottled rusty brown above and grayish below, with white barring along the belly and sides. The head has a black patch between the eye and bill, and the bill is yellow and conical. The tail is pointed and often cocked up and flicked. The juvenile is pale brown below, with less black on the face. Soras feed along shorelines or at the edges of meadows for snails, insects, and aquatic plants. Their voice is a soft, rising *Ooo-eep*, and they are quite tame, being seen more often than other rails. (Illustration shows a breeding adult.)

**Sandhill Crane,** *Grus canadensis*
Family Gruidae (Cranes)
**Size:** 45″
**Season:** Spring and fall during migration
**Habitat:** Fields, shallow wetlands

The Sandhill Crane is a tall bird with long, strong legs, a long neck, and a long, straight bill. The long, thick tertial feathers create the distinctive bustle on the rear of all cranes. The top of the Sandhill Crane's head is covered by red, bare skin. Plumage is gray overall, but may become spotted with rust-colored stains caused by preening with a bill stained by iron-rich mud. In flocks, the crane grazes in fields gleaning grains, insects, and small animals, then returns to roost in protected wetland areas. The voice of the Sandhill Crane is a throaty, penetrating, trumpeting sound. Unlike herons, it flies in groups with its neck extended. (Illustration shows an adult.)

### Killdeer, *Charadrius vociferus*
Family Charadriidae (Plovers)
**Size:** 10"
**Season:** Summer
**Habitat:** Inland fields, farmlands, lakeshores, meadows

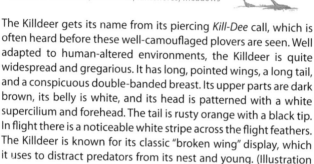

The Killdeer gets its name from its piercing *Kill-Dee* call, which is often heard before these well-camouflaged plovers are seen. Well adapted to human-altered environments, the Killdeer is quite widespread and gregarious. It has long, pointed wings, a long tail, and a conspicuous double-banded breast. Its upper parts are dark brown, its belly is white, and its head is patterned with a white supercilium and forehead. The tail is rusty orange with a black tip. In flight there is a noticeable white stripe across the flight feathers. The Killdeer is known for its classic "broken wing" display, which it uses to distract predators from its nest and young. (Illustration shows an adult.)

### American Avocet,
*Recurvirostra americana*
Family Recurvirostridae (Avocets, Stilts)
**Size:** 18"
**Season:** Summer
**Habitat:** Shallow wetlands, marshes

The elegant American Avocet has a long, delicate, black, upturned bill and long, thin, blue-gray legs. The upperparts are patterned black and white, the belly is white, and the head and neck is light orange-brown punctuated by black eyes. The bill of the female is slightly shorter than that of the male, with a greater bend. Nonbreeding adults have a pale gray head and neck. Avocets use a side-to-side sweeping motion with their bills to stir up small crustaceans and insect larvae as they wade methodically through the shallows. They may even submerge their heads as the water deepens. They are adept swimmers and emit a *Wheet!* call in alarm. (Illustration shows a breeding male, below, and a female, above.)

## Greater Yellowlegs,
*Tringa melanoleuca*
Family Scolopacidae (Sandpipers, Phalaropes)
**Size:** 14"
**Season:** Summer
**Habitat:** Marshes

The Greater Yellowlegs is sometimes called the "tell-tale" bird, as the sentinel of a flock raises an alarm when danger is near, flying off and circling to return. It has long, bright yellow legs, a long neck, a dark, slightly upturned bill, and a white eye ring. The upperparts are dark gray and mottled, while the underparts are white with barring on the flanks. In breeding plumage the barring is noticeably darker and more extensive. To feed, the Greater Yellowlegs strides forward actively to pick small aquatic prey from the water or to chase fish. The Lesser Yellowlegs is similar but smaller. (Illustration shows a nonbreeding adult.)

## Spotted Sandpiper, *Actitus macularius*
Family Scolopacidae (Sandpipers, Phalaropes)
**Size:** 7½"
**Season:** Summer
**Habitat:** Creek sides, edges of lakes and ponds

The solitary Spotted Sandpiper is known for its exaggerated, constant bobbing motion. It has a compact body, a long tail, and a short neck and legs. Plumage is brown above and light below, with a white shoulder patch. There is a white eye ring and superciliary stripe above the dark eye line. In breeding plumage the Spotted Sandpiper develops heavy spotting from the chin to lower flanks and barring on the back. Its bill is orange with a dark tip. It has short wings, and in flight a thin white stripe on the upper wing is visible. To forage, the sandpiper teeters about, picking small water prey and insects from along the shoreline. (Illustration shows a breeding adult.)

## Long-billed Curlew,
*Numenius americanus*
Family Scolopacidae (Sandpipers, Phalaropes)
**Size:** 23"
**Season:** Summer in eastern Colorado
**Habitat:** Open grasslands, mudflats, lakeside beaches

Sometimes called the Sicklebill, the Long-billed Curlew is Colorado's largest curlew, with an extremely long, thin, decurved bill (longer in females than in males). It is mottled gray-brown above, with buff underparts. Facial markings are not pronounced, and the undersides of the wings are a rich cinnamon color. It strides ahead in a deliberate manner with its head forward, picking or probing for crustaceans and insects. Its large eyes enable it to feed in the dark hours of early morning. The curlew's voice is a loud, ringing *Kur-Lee!* (Illustration shows an adult.)

## Common Snipe, *Gallinago gallinago*
Family Scolopacidae (Sandpipers, Phalaropes)
**Size:** 10½"
**Season:** Year-round
**Habitat:** Salt- or freshwater marshes

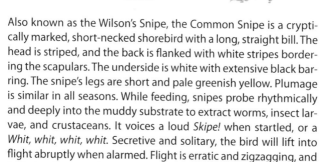

Also known as the Wilson's Snipe, the Common Snipe is a cryptically marked, short-necked shorebird with a long, straight bill. The head is striped, and the back is flanked with white stripes bordering the scapulars. The underside is white with extensive black barring. The snipe's legs are short and pale greenish yellow. Plumage is similar in all seasons. While feeding, snipes probe rhythmically and deeply into the muddy substrate to extract worms, insect larvae, and crustaceans. It voices a loud *Skipe!* when startled, or a *Whit, whit, whit, whit.* Secretive and solitary, the bird will lift into flight abruptly when alarmed. Flight is erratic and zigzagging, and includes displays of "winnowing," where air across the tail feathers whistles during a steep descent. (Illustration shows an adult.)

## Wilson's Phalarope, *Phalaropus tricolor*
Family Scolopacidae (Sandpipers, Phalaropes)
**Size:** 9"
**Season:** Summer
**Habitat:** Shallow pools around grassy or muddy wetlands

The Wilson's Phalarope is a small, thin, elegant shorebird with a relatively long neck and a long, needlelike black bill. With phalaropes, the female is the more brightly colored sex. In breeding plumage the female has a gray-brown back, clean white underparts, and a pale orange-brown throat. A thin, black stripe runs from the bill, across the eye, and down the neck to the back. The head has pale cheeks and a gray crown, and the legs are black. Winter plumage is pale gray above and white below, and the legs are yellow. The breeding male looks like the winter adult female, with a dark eye stripe, crown, and nape. The Wilson's Phalarope actively walks along shorelines or swims in circles to find insects or plant material. (Illustration shows a breeding female, below, and a breeding male, above.)

## Bonaparte's Gull,
*Chroicocephalus philadelphia*
Family Laridae (Gulls, Terns)
**Size:** 13"
**Season:** Fall and spring migrant
**Habitat:** Lakes, wetlands

The Bonaparte's Gull is a small gull named after an American ornithologist who was related to Napoleon. It is agile and ternlike in flight, skimming low over the water to snatch fish. It has a thin, sharp, black bill and red legs. Plumage in breeding season includes a black head that contrasts with its white body and light gray back and wings. The primaries form a white triangle against the dark trailing edge when the gull is in flight. The nonbreeding adult has a mostly white head, with black eyes and small dark spots around the ears. A solitary gull, the Bonaparte does not form large flocks. It builds nests made of sticks in evergreen trees. (Illustration shows a breeding adult, below, and a nonbreeding adult, above.)

## Ring-billed Gull,
*Larus delewarensis*
Family Laridae (Gulls, Terns)
**Size:** 18"
**Season:** Winter; transient in spring and fall
**Habitat:** Lakes, ponds, parking lots

The Ring-billed Gull is common and quite tame. It is a relatively small gull with a rounded white head and a yellow bill with a dark subterminal ring. It has a pale gray back with black primaries tipped with white, and white underparts. Its eyes are pale yellow, and its legs are yellow as well. The nonbreeding adult has faint streaking on the nape and around the eyes. Ring-billed Gulls feed on the water or on the ground, taking a wide variety of foodstuffs, and may scavenge in urban areas and dumps. (Illustration shows a nonbreeding adult.)

## Herring Gull, *Larus argentatus*
Family Laridae (Gulls, Terns)
**Size:** 25"
**Season:** Winter; transient in spring and fall
**Habitat:** Wetlands, lakeshores, fields

The widespread Herring Gull occurs across the North American continent. It is large, relatively thin, and white-headed with a pale gray back and white underparts. The bill is thick and yellow with a reddish spot at the tip of the lower mandible. The primaries are black with white-spotted tips. The nonbreeding adult has brown streaking across the nape and neck. The gull's legs are pink and the eyes are pale yellow to ivory colored. The Herring Gull is an opportunistic feeder, eating fish, worms, crumbs, and trash. It is known to drop shellfish from the air to crack open the shells. (Illustration shows a breeding adult, below, and a nonbreeding adult, above.)

GULLS, TERNS

### California Gull, *Larus californicus*
Family Laridae (Gulls, Terns)
**Size:** 21"
**Season:** Summer; transient in spring and fall
**Habitat:** Lakes, rivers, prairie wetlands

The California Gull is a medium-size gull with a relatively thin, long bill. The breeding adult is medium blue-gray above, with white edges to the tertials and secondaries, and is white below. The primaries are black with white spotting, and the tail is white. The head is rounded, the eyes are dark, and the bill is yellow-orange with a black-and-red spot near the tip. The legs are greenish yellow. Winter adults show brownish streaking on the nape. California Gulls breed in large colonies, and feed on a variety of food including fish, small mammals, and insects. The gull's voice is a harsh squawk. (Illustration shows a breeding adult.)

### Forster's Tern, *Sterna forsteri*
Family Laridae (Gulls, Terns)
**Size:** 14"
**Season:** Summer
**Habitat:** Lakes, marshes

The Forster's Tern is a medium-size tern with no crest and a relatively long, pointed, orange bill with a black tip. Breeding plumage is very pale gray above and white below, with a white forked tail and very light primaries. The head has a black cap, and the short legs are red. Nonbreeding adults have darker primaries, a black ear patch in place of the cap, and a black bill. Forster's Terns display swallowlike flight, with narrow pointed wings, and they plunge-dive for fish. They voice short, harsh, one-syllable calls. (Illustration shows a breeding adult, below, and a nonbreeding adult, above.)

### Black Tern, *Childonias niger*
Family Laridae (Gulls, Terns)
**Size:** 9½"
**Season:** Summer; transient in spring and fall
**Habitat:** Wet meadows, marshes, fields

The Black Tern is a small, dark tern with a very short, notched tail, and a small, thin, black bill. The breeding adult is dark gray above and black below, with white undertail coverts and vent. The head is all black, and there is a hint of red at the gape. The tern's non-breeding plumage is lighter gray above and all white below, with a white head except for black around the eye and at the rear of the crown. Black Terns fly low over water, or circle and hover, dropping down to capture insects, fish, and invertebrates. They do not plunge-dive like other terns. (Illustration shows a breeding adult.)

### Mourning Dove, *Zenaida macroura*
Family Columbidae (Pigeons, Doves)
**Size:** 12"
**Season:** Year-round
**Habitat:** Open brushy areas, urban areas

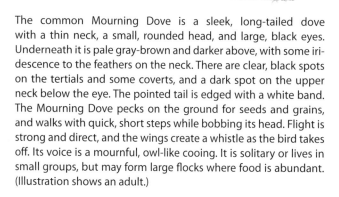

The common Mourning Dove is a sleek, long-tailed dove with a thin neck, a small, rounded head, and large, black eyes. Underneath it is pale gray-brown and darker above, with some iridescence to the feathers on the neck. There are clear, black spots on the tertials and some coverts, and a dark spot on the upper neck below the eye. The pointed tail is edged with a white band. The Mourning Dove pecks on the ground for seeds and grains, and walks with quick, short steps while bobbing its head. Flight is strong and direct, and the wings create a whistle as the bird takes off. Its voice is a mournful, owl-like cooing. It is solitary or lives in small groups, but may form large flocks where food is abundant. (Illustration shows an adult.)

35

### Rock Dove (Pigeon),
*Columba livia*
Family Columbidae (Pigeons, Doves)
**Size:** 12"
**Season:** Year-round
**Habitat:** Urban areas, farmland

The Rock Dove is the common pigeon seen in almost every urban area across the continent. Introduced from Europe, where they inhabit rocky cliffs, Rock Doves have adapted to city life, and domestication has resulted in a huge variety of plumage colors and patterns. The original, wild version is a stocky, gray bird with a darker head and neck, and green to purple iridescence along the sides of the neck. The eye is bright red, and the bill has a fleshy, white cere on the base of the upper mandible. There are two dark bars across the back when the wing is folded, the rump is white, and the tail has a dark terminal band. Variants range from white to brown to black, with many pattern combinations. (Illustration shows an adult.)

### Band-tailed Pigeon,
*Patagioenas fasciata*
Family Columbidae (Pigeons, Doves)
**Size:** 14"
**Season:** Summer
**Habitat:** Mountainous pine woodlands, urban areas (sometimes)

The Band-tailed Pigeon is the largest pigeon, and has a heavy body with a relatively long tail and small, rounded head. Plumage is medium brownish gray overall, with darker wings and a purplish brown cast to the breast. The bill is yellow with a black tip, the eye is dark with a red orbital ring, and the nape is iridescent green and bordered above by a thin, white band. The outer half of the tail has a broad, pale band. Band-tailed Pigeons consume a varied diet of insects, seeds, and berries, and voice a low, owl-like, two-part *Hoo-Hoooo*. (Illustration shows an adult.)

### Yellow-billed Cuckoo,
*Coccyzus americanus*
Family Cuculidae (Cuckoos)
**Size:** 12"
**Season:** Summer in eastern Colorado
**Habitat:** Streamsides, swamps,
a variety of woodlands

Like other cuckoos, the Yellow-billed Cuckoo is secretive and shy,
hiding in vegetation where it picks insects, caterpillars, and fruit
from trees. It is brown above with rufous flight feathers, and crisp
white below. The bill is yellow with black along the top ridge. The
tail is long and gradated, with large white spots on the underside.
(Illustration shows an adult.)

CUCKOOS

### Greater Roadrunner,
*Geococcyx californianus*
Family Cuculidae (Cuckoos)
**Size:** 23"
**Season:** Year-round in south-
eastern Colorado
**Habitat:** Open fields, grasslands,
urban areas

The Greater Roadrunner is a very large, ground-dwelling cuckoo
with rounded wings, a long tail and neck, and a strong, pointed
bill. It is heavily streaked overall, except for a pale gray belly. A
pale blue patch appears behind the eye, and its short, shaggy
crest is often raised. Its legs are long and sturdy. Roadrunners
run with their tails held horizontal and their necks outstretched,
and rarely fly. They forage by chasing down reptiles, insects, and
rodents. Their call is a deep cooing. (Illustration shows an adult.)

### Great Horned Owl,
*Bubo virginianus*
Family Strigidae (Typical Owls)
**Size:** 22"
**Season:** Year-round
**Habitat:** Almost any environment, from forests to plains to urban areas

Found throughout North America, the Great Horned Owl is a large, strong owl with an obvious facial disk and sharp, long talons. Plumage is variable: Eastern forms are brown overall with heavy barring, a rust-colored face, and a white chin patch, while western forms are grayer. The prominent ear tufts give the owl its name, and the eyes are large and yellow. The Great Horned Owl has exceptional hearing and sight. It feeds at night, perching on branches or posts, then swooping down on silent wings to catch birds, snakes, or mammals up to the size of a cat. Its voice is a low *Hoo-Hoo-Hoo*. (Illustration shows an adult.)

### Burrowing Owl, *Athene cunicularia*
Family Strigidae (Typical Owls)
**Size:** 9½"
**Season:** Summer
**Habitat:** Open grasslands and plains

The Burrowing Owl is a ground-dwelling owl that lives in burrows that have been vacated by rodents or tortoises. It is small and flat-headed, and has a short tail and long legs. Plumage above is brown spotted with white, and extensively barred brown and white below. It has a white chin and throat, and bright yellow eyes. Burrowing Owls can be seen day or night perched on the ground or on posts, scanning for insects and small rodents. Sometimes they exhibit a bowing movement when approached. The voice is a chattering or cooing, and sometimes imitative of a rattlesnake. (Illustration shows an adult.)

## Western Screech Owl,
*Megascops kennicottii*
Family Strigidae (Typical Owls)
**Size:** 8½"
**Season:** Year-round in western Colorado
**Habitat:** Wooded areas or parks; places where cavity-bearing trees exist

The Western Screech Owl is a small, eared owl with a big head, short tail, and bright yellow eyes. The highly camouflaged plumage ranges from brown to gray, depending on the region. It is darker above, streaked and barred below. The ear tufts may be drawn back to give the appearance of a rounded head, and the bill is grayish green tipped with white. White spots on the margins of the coverts and scapulars create two white bars on the folded wing. It is a nocturnal bird, hunting during the night for small mammals, insects, or fish. Its voice is a descending, whistling call or a rapid staccato of one pitch. (Illustration shows an adult.)

## Common Poorwill,
*Phalaenoptilus nuttallii*
Family Caprimulgidae (Nightjars, Nighthawks)
**Size:** 8"
**Season:** Summer
**Habitat:** Rocky areas, arid plains and shrubland

The Common Poorwill is a very small nightjar with an oversize head, rounded wings, and a very short, stubby tail. Plumage is cryptically mottled and barred grayish overall, with a white chin stripe and darker areas around the eye and upper breast. The outer edges of the tail are white, and the wings are brown with dark barring. The tiny bill is based with heavy whiskers. From a ground perch, Common Poorwills flutter up to catch insects in flight. They are mostly nocturnal and ground dwelling, and may even hibernate during winter months. (Illustration shows an adult.)

## Common Nighthawk,
*Chordeiles minor*
Family Caprimulgidae (Nightjars, Nighthawks)
**Size:** 9"
**Season:** Summer
**Habitat:** Forests, marshes, plains, urban areas

SWIFTS

The Common Nighthawk is primarily nocturnal, but may be seen flying during the day and evening hours, catching insects on the wing with bounding flight. It is cryptically mottled gray, brown, and black, with strong barring on an otherwise pale underside. In the male a white breast band is evident. The tail is long and slightly notched, and the wings are long and pointed, extending past the tail in the perched bird. In flight there is a distinct white patch on both sides of the wings. During the day the Common Nighthawk is usually seen roosting on posts or branches with its eyes closed. Its voice is a short, nasal, buzzing sound. (Illustration shows an adult male.)

## Chimney Swift,
*Chaetura pelagica*
Family Apodidae (Swifts)
**Size:** 5"
**Season:** Summer in eastern Colorado
**Habitat:** Woods, scrub, swamps, urban areas

The gregarious Chimney Swift is unrelated to the swallows but similar in shape. Its body is like a fat torpedo, with a very short tail and long, pointed, bowed wings that bend close to the body. It is dark brown overall, slightly paler underneath and at the chin. Constantly on the wing, it catches insects in flight with quick wing beats and fast glides. It never perches, but roosts at night on vertical cliffs, trees, or in chimneys. Its voice is a quick chattering uttered in flight. (Illustration shows an adult.)

## White-throated Swift,
*Aeronautes saxatalis*
Family Apodidae (Swifts)
**Size:** 6"
**Season:** Summer
**Habitat:** Areas near cliffs, crevices, and canyons

The White-throated Swift is a large, speedy swift with swooping, pointed wings and a slightly forked tail. It is black overall, with crisp white patches along the belly, on the sides of the rump, and on the lower half of the head, extending above the eye. In swifts the wings are bent near the body, unlike swallows where the bend is farther out. A highly aerial bird, it spends most of the day in flight, reaching incredible speeds using fast wing beats, and gliding high in the air. It roosts in cracks and crevices during the night. (Illustration shows an adult.)

## Black-chinned Hummingbird,
*Archilochus alexandri*
Family Trochilidae (Hummingbirds)
**Size:** 3½"
**Season:** Summer in eastern Colorado
**Habitat:** Riparian areas in woodlands, canyons, areas with oak trees

The Black-chinned Hummingbird is a small, delicate bird able to hover on wings that beat at a blinding speed. The long, needle-like bill is used to probe deep into flowers so the bird can lap up nectar. Its feet are tiny. The body is white below and green above. Males have a dark green crown and an iridescent violet and black throat, or gorget. Females lack the colored gorget and have a light green crown and white-tipped tail feathers. Its behavior is typical of hummingbirds, hovering and buzzing from flower to flower, emitting chits and squeaks. Most of these birds migrate across the Gulf of Mexico to South America in the winter. (Illustration shows a male, below, and a female, above.)

## Rufous Hummingbird,
*Selasphorus rufus*
Family Trochilidae (Hummingbirds)
**Size:** 3½"
**Season:** Spring and fall during migration
**Habitat:** Woodlands, parks, gardens

The Rufous Hummingbird is a small, compact hummingbird with a relatively short bill and short wings. The male is bright rufous orange with green wings, a white breast patch, and an iridescent bronze gorget (throat patch). The tail is tipped with black. Females have white tips on the outer tail feathers, a green back and crown, and a whitish chin with rufous spotting that sometimes forms a congealed spot in the middle. Rufous Hummingbirds drink nectar from flowers and feeders, and sometimes eat small insects. (Illustration shows a male, below, and a female, above.)

## Belted Kingfisher, *Megaceryle alcyon*
Family Alcedinidae (Kingfishers)
**Size:** 13"
**Season:** Year-round
**Habitat:** Creeks, lakes

The widespread but solitary Belted Kingfisher is a stocky, large-headed bird with a long, powerful bill and shaggy crest. It is grayish blue-green above and white below, with a thick blue band across the breast and white dotting on the back. White spots are at the lores. The female has an extra breast band of rufous hue, and is rufous along the flanks. Belted Kingfishers feed by springing from a perch along the water's edge or by hovering above the water, then plunging headfirst to snatch fish, frogs, or tadpoles. Flight is uneven, and its vocalization is a raspy, rattling sound. (Illustration shows an adult female.)

### Red-headed Woodpecker,
*Melanerpes erythrocephalus*
Family Picidae (Woodpeckers)
**Size:** 9"
**Season:** Summer in eastern Colorado
**Habitat:** Woodlands, suburbs, areas with standing dead trees

The Red-headed Woodpecker has a striking bright red head and a powerful tapered bill. It is black above, with a large patch of white across the lower back and secondaries, and is white below. The juvenile has a pale brown head and an incomplete white back patch. In all woodpeckers the tail is very stiff, with sharp tips that help support the bird while it clings to a tree trunk. To feed, it pecks at bark for insects, but may also fly out to snatch its prey in midair. Nuts will also be taken and stored in tree cavities for winter. This species has been losing nesting cavities since the introduction of the European Starling. (Illustration shows an adult.)

### Lewis's Woodpecker, *Melanerpes lewis*
Family Picidae (Woodpeckers)
**Size:** 11"
**Season:** Year-round
**Habitat:** Open woodlands, streamsides

The Lewis's Woodpecker is large and mostly dark. Plumage is greenish black above and gray below, fading to a dusky rose color on the belly. The gray of the breast continues around the neck to form a light collar. The head is dark: deep red in front surrounded by greenish black plumage. The long, stiff tail feathers support the bird while it is perched on vertical trunks. In flight, Lewis's Woodpeckers are steady and direct, not undulating like most woodpeckers. From a perch on the tree trunk, they fly out to catch insects, or eat nuts that they have stored in cavities. They are often seen in groups. (Illustration shows an adult.)

## Red-naped Sapsucker,
*Sphyrapicus nuchalis*
Family Picidae (Woodpeckers)
**Size:** 8½"
**Season:** Summer
**Habitat:** Woodlands, suburbs, areas with standing dead trees

The sapsuckers are named for their habit of drilling rows of pits in tree bark, then returning to eat the sap that emerges and the insects that come to investigate. They will also flycatch and eat berries. The Red-naped Sapsucker is medium-size, with pied black-and-white plumage and barring across the back. The head is boldly patterned in black and white, with a red crown and red chin (white in females). The belly is unbarred and pale yellow, while the flanks are white with black barring. In flight there is a distinct white patch on the upper wing. This bird was once considered the same species as the eastern Yellow-bellied Sapsucker. (Illustration shows an adult male.)

2/15/15

## Downy Woodpecker, *Picoides pubescens*
Family Picidae (Woodpeckers)
**Size:** 6½"
**Season:** Year-round
**Habitat:** Woodlands, parks, urban areas, streamsides

The Downy Woodpecker is a tiny woodpecker with a small bill and a relatively large head. It is white underneath with no barring, has black wings barred with white, and a patch of white on its back. The head is boldly patterned in white and black, and the male sports a red nape patch. The base of the bill joins the head with fluffy nasal tufts. Juveniles may show some red on the forehead and crown. It forages for berries and insects in the bark and among the smaller twigs of trees. The very similar Hairy Woodpecker is larger, with a longer bill and more aggressive foraging behavior, sticking to larger branches and not clinging to twigs. (Illustration shows an adult male.)

Pecking around a tree outside the living room window

## Hairy Woodpecker,
*Picoides villosus*
Family Picidae (Woodpeckers)
**Size:** 9"
**Season:** Year-round
**Habitat:** Mixed woodlands, creek sides near large trees

The Hairy Woodpecker is very similar in plumage to the Downy Woodpecker, but is larger with a heavier bill. Also, it pecks for insects in tree bark or on larger branches, and will not feed from smaller twigs as does the Downy. It is mostly black above, with a white patch on its back and outer tail feathers, and some white spotting on the wings. The underside is white with no barring. The head is patterned in black and white, there are small nasal tufts, and males show a red patch on the back of the crown. The woodpecker's voice includes a high-pitched, squeaky *Chip, Chip,* as well as loud drumming. (Illustration shows an adult female.)

## Northern Flicker, *Colaptes auratus*
Family Picidae (Woodpeckers)
**Size:** 12½"
**Season:** Year-round
**Habitat:** Variety of habitats including suburbs and parks

The common Northern Flicker is a large, long-tailed woodpecker often seen foraging on the ground for ants and other small insects. It is barred brown and black across the back above, and buff with black spotting below. The head is brown with a gray nape and crown. On the upper breast is a prominent half-circle of black, and the male has a red patch at the malar region. Flight is undulating and shows an orange wing lining and white rump. The flicker's voice is a loud, sharp *Keee,* and it will sometimes drum its bill repeatedly at objects, like a jackhammer. It is sometimes referred to as the Red-shafted Flicker. (Illustration shows an adult male.)

# PASSERINES

## Olive-sided Flycatcher, *Contopus cooperi*
Family Tyrannidae (Tyrant Flycatchers)
**Size:** 7½"
**Season:** Summer
**Habitat:** Open coniferous woodlands

The Olive-sided Flycatcher is a stocky flycatcher with a relatively large head, a thick neck, and a short, slightly notched tail. It is dark olive gray above, on the head, and on the sides, with a white strip that runs down the middle of the belly and up to the chin, forming a sort of "vest" shape. The sides of the rump are white, but this is usually concealed in the perched bird. The bill is stout, thick at the base, and pointed. It perches on high, bare, treetop branches and flycatches for insects. Its voice is a high-pitched *Whip Wee Weer,* sometimes dubbed *Quick Three Beers.* (Illustration shows an adult.)

## Western Wood-Pewee, *Contopus sordidulus*
Family Tyrannidae (Tyrant Flycatchers)
**Size:** 6¼"
**Season:** Summer
**Habitat:** Woodland edges, canyons, creek sides

The Western Wood-Pewee is a large-headed, thick-necked flycatcher with drab plumage overall. It is brownish gray or olive gray, with pale whitish or dusky underparts and gray sides that meet at the breast. A very slight eye ring surrounds the dark eye, and the bill is thin, pointed, and has a pale lower mandible. There are thin wing bars along the coverts and edges of the tertials. It is nearly identical to the Eastern Wood-Pewee, but the ranges do not normally overlap. Western Wood-Pewees flycatch for insects, starting from a high perch and then returning to the same spot. The voice is composed of shrill, high-pitched *Pee-Wee* notes. (Illustration shows an adult.)

## Willow Flycatcher,
*Empidonax traillii*
Family Tyrannidae (Tyrant Flycatchers)
**Size:** 5¾"
**Season:** Summer
**Habitat:** Moist, brushy areas with willows, foothill fields

The Willow Flycatcher is similar to many flycatchers in the genus *Empidonax*. It has a crown that peaks at the rear of the head, and a fairly thick bill. Plumage is greenish brown-gray above, with pale, dusky underparts and a whitish chin and throat. Around the eye is a thin white eye ring. The lores are light, and the lower mandible is pale orange. Distinct wing bars are visible on the folded wing. Willow Flycatchers catch insects, starting from a perch and returning to the same spot. The vocalization is a high, nasal *Fitz-Bee* call. (Illustration shows an adult.)

## Say's Phoebe, *Sayornis saya*
Family Tyrannidae (Tyrant Flycatchers)
**Size:** 7½"
**Season:** Summer
**Habitat:** Arid open country, shrubland

The Say's Phoebe is a fairly slim flycatcher with a long, black tail. It is pale gray-brown above, with lighter wings bars. The underside is whitish to gray under the chin and breast, fading to orange-brown on the belly and undertail coverts. The head has a flat crown that often peaks toward the rear, and the bird has dark eyes, lores, and bill. It flycatches for insects from a perch on rocks or twigs. The Say's Phoebe voices a high, whistled *Pit-Eur*, and often pumps or flares out its tail. (Illustration shows an adult.)

## Western Kingbird, *Tyrannus verticalis*
Family Tyrannidae (Tyrant Flycatchers)
**Size:** 8¾"
**Season:** Summer
**Habitat:** Open fields, agricultural areas

The Western Kingbird is a relatively slender flycatcher with a stout, black bill and a slightly rounded, black tail with white along the outer edge. It is grayish or greenish brown above, pale gray on the breast, and bright yellow on the belly, sides, and undertail coverts. The head is light gray with a white throat and malar area, and dark gray at the lores and behind the eye. There is a small, reddish crown patch that is normally concealed. Western Kingbirds flycatch for insects from perches on branches, posts, or wires, and the voice is composed of quick, high-pitched zips and chits. (Illustration shows an adult.)

TYRANT FLYCATCHERS

## Eastern Kingbird,
*Tyrannus tyrannus*
Family Tyrannidae (Tyrant Flycatchers)
**Size:** 8½"
**Season:** Summer
**Habitat:** Open woodlands, agricultural and rural areas

The Eastern Kingbird is a slender, medium-size flycatcher. Its upperparts are bluish black, and its underparts are white with a pale gray breast. The dark head cap contrasts with the white lower half of the face. The tail is black with a white terminal band. It flies with shallow wing beats on wings that are mostly dark and pointed. Eastern Kingbirds perch on wires, treetops, or posts and take flight to capture insects on the wing. The voice is a distinctive series of very high-pitched, sputtering, zippy *Psit* notes. (Illustration shows an adult.)

## Loggerhead Shrike,
*Lanius ludovicianus*
Family Laniidae (Shrikes)
**Size:** 9½"
**Season:** Year-round in southern Colorado; summer elsewhere
**Habitat:** Dry open country with perches including branches, wires, and posts

The solitary Loggerhead Shrike is raptorlike in its feeding habits. It captures large insects, small mammals, or birds and impales them on thorny barbs before tearing them apart to feed. It is a compact, large-headed bird with a short, thick, slightly hooked bill. Its upperparts are gray and its underparts are pale. The wings are black with white patches at the base of the primaries and upper coverts. The tail is black and edged with white. There is a black mask on the head, extending from the base of the bill to the ear area. Juveniles show a finely barred breast. The shrike's flight is composed of quick wing beats and swooping glides. (Illustration shows an adult.)

## Red-eyed Vireo, *Vireo olivaceus*
Family Vireonidae (Vireos)
**Size:** 6"
**Season:** Summer in eastern Colorado
**Habitat:** Areas of dense vegetation; mature deciduous forests

The Red-eyed Vireo is a sluggish, slow-moving bird that haunts the upper tree canopy picking out insects and berries. Its head appears rather flat and its tail is short. It is light olive green above and white below, with a yellow wash across the breast, flanks, and undertail coverts. It has a dark eye line, white eyebrow, and a grayish crown. The eyes are red, and the bill is fairly large with a hooked tip. The voice is a repetitive, incessant song in single phrases. (Illustration shows an adult.)

### Warbling Vireo, *Vireo gilvus*
Family Vireonidae (Vireos)
**Size:** 5½"
**Season:** Summer
**Habitat:** Moist deciduous woodland, parks

The Warbling Vireo is a plain, light-colored, stocky vireo with a fairly short, hooked bill. The upperparts are pale brownish or greenish gray with no distinct wing bars, and the underside is whitish or washed with pale yellow-brown. The dark eyes contrast with the light superciliary stripes and lores. The underside of the wing is two-toned, with light linings and darker flight feathers. Warbling Vireos forage in trees for insects and berries, and sing a high-pitched, warbling song. (Illustration shows an adult.)

### Blue Jay, *Cyanocitta cristata*
Family Corvidae (Jays, Crows)
**Size:** 11"
**Season:** Year-round in northeastern Colorado
**Habitat:** Woodlands, rural and urban areas

The solitary Blue Jay is a sturdy, crested jay. It is bright blue above and white below, with a thick, tapered, black bill. There is a white patch around the eye that extends to the chin, bordered by a thin, black "necklace" extending to the nape. It has a conspicuous white wing bar and dark barring on the wings and tail. In flight the white outer edges of the tail are visible. The jay alternates shallow wing beats with glides. Omnivorous, the Blue Jay eats just about anything, especially acorns, nuts, fruits, insects, and small vertebrates. It is a raucous and noisy bird and quite bold. Sometimes it mimics the calls of birds of prey. (Illustration shows an adult.)

## Steller's Jay, *Cyanocitta stelleri*
Family Corvidae (Jays, Crows)
**Size:** 11½"
**Season:** Year-round
**Habitat:** Coniferous forests,
mountainous areas

The Steller's Jay is a bold, stocky, crested jay with short, broad wings. The tail, back, wings, and belly are bright deep blue, while the mantle and breast are sooty gray. The black head has a thick, pointed crest, and inland races have white eyebrows and thin, white streaks on the forehead. The legs and bill are stout and strong. Steller's Jays eat a wide variety of food, from nuts, insects, and berries to picnic scraps. Their voice is a loud, raucous squawking, and they sometimes mimic the calls of other birds. (Illustration shows an adult.)

## Western Scrub-Jay,
*Aphelocoma californica*
Family Corvidae (Jays, Crows)
**Size:** 11½"
**Season:** Year-round
**Habitat:** Open areas of scrub oak,
urban areas

The Western Scrub-Jay is a long-necked, sleek, crestless jay. Its upperparts are deep blue, with a distinct, lighter, gray-brown mantle. Its underparts are pale gray, becoming white on the belly and undertail coverts. There is a thin, white superciliary stripe, the malar area is dark gray, and the throat is streaked with white and gray above a dull gray "necklace" across the breast. The bird's flight is an undulating combination of rapid wing beats and swooping glides. Its diet consists of nuts, seeds, insects, and fruit. (Illustration shows an adult.)

### Pinyon Jay,
*Gymnorhinus cyanocephalus*
Family Corvidae (Jays, Crows)
**Size:** 10½"
**Season:** Year-round
**Habitat:** Juniper-pinyon scrub, open pine forests

The Pinyon Jay is a highly social, plain-colored, crestless jay with a short, squarish tail and a thin, pointed bill. Plumage is pale gray-blue overall, and even paler underneath. The head is a brighter blue, with dark lores, and the throat is streaked with pale gray. Pinyon Jays favor the nuts from the pinyon pine, as well as berries and other seeds. They voice a nasal, loud *Caw-Caw-Caw*. They form huge feeding flocks and breeding colonies. Their flight is direct, without undulations. (Illustration shows an adult.)

### Clark's Nutcracker, *Nucifraga columbiana*
Family Corvidae (Jays, Crows)
**Size:** 12"
**Season:** Year-round
**Habitat:** Coniferous forests of high mountain areas

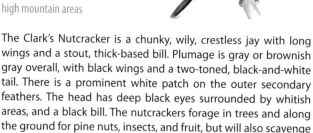

The Clark's Nutcracker is a chunky, wily, crestless jay with long wings and a stout, thick-based bill. Plumage is gray or brownish gray overall, with black wings and a two-toned, black-and-white tail. There is a prominent white patch on the outer secondary feathers. The head has deep black eyes surrounded by whitish areas, and a black bill. The nutcrackers forage in trees and along the ground for pine nuts, insects, and fruit, but will also scavenge at picnic grounds. Clark's Nutcrackers walk with a swaying, crow-like gait, and voice loud, harsh, rattling squawks. (Illustration shows an adult.)

**Black-billed Magpie,** *Pica hudsonia*  1/27/15
Family Corvidae (Jays, Crows)
**Size:** 19"
**Season:** Year-round
**Habitat:** Riparian areas, open woodlands, pastures, rural areas

The Black-billed Magpie is a heavy, broad-winged bird with an extremely long, graduated tail. It has striking pied plumage, being black on the head, upper breast, and back, dark iridescent green-blue on the wings and tail, and crisp white on the scapulars and belly. The legs are dark and stout, and the bill is thick at the base. Juvenile birds have a much shorter tail. Magpies travel in small groups, and are opportunistic feeders of insects, nuts, eggs, or carrion. The voice is a whining, questioning *Mag?* or a harsh *Wok-Wok.* (Illustration shows an adult.)

**American Crow,**
*Corvus brachyrhynchus*
Family Corvidae (Jays, Crows)
**Size:** 17½"
**Season:** Year-round
**Habitat:** Open woodlands, pastures, rural fields, dumps

The American Crow is a widespread corvid found across the continent. Known for its familiar, loud, grating *Caw, caw* vocalization, the crow is a large, stocky bird with a short, rounded tail, broad wings, and a thick, powerful bill. Plumage is glistening black overall, in all stages of development. It will eat almost anything, and often forms loose flocks with other crows. (Illustration shows an adult.)

## Common Raven, *Corvus corax*
Family Corvidae (Jays, Crows)
**Size:** 24"
**Season:** Year-round
**Habitat:** Wide range of habitats including deserts, mountains, canyons, and forests

The Common Raven is a stocky, gruff, large corvid with a long, massive bill that slopes directly into the forehead. The wings are narrow and long, and the tail is rounded or wedge-shaped. The entire body is glossy black, sometimes bluish, and the neck is laced with pointed, shaggy feathers. Quite omnivorous, it feeds on carrion, refuse, insects, and roadkill, and has a varied voice that includes deep croaking. Ravens may soar and engage in rather acrobatic flight. Crows are similar but are smaller, with proportionately smaller bills. (Illustration shows an adult.)

## Horned Lark, *Eremophila alpestris*
Family Alaudidae (Larks)
**Size:** 7"
**Season:** Year-round
**Habitat:** Open and barren country

The Horned Lark is a slim, elongated, ground-dwelling bird with long wings. The plumage is pale reddish gray above and whitish below, with variable amounts of rusty smudging or streaking on the breast and sides. The head is boldly patterned with a black crown, cheek patch, and breast bar, contrasting with a yellow throat and white face. In females the black markings are much paler. Particularly evident on males, there are feather tufts, or "horns," on the sides of the crown. Outer tail feathers are black. Horned Larks scurry on the ground, foraging for plant matter and insects, and sing with rapid, musical warbles and chips. (Illustration shows an adult male.)

## Purple Martin, *Progne subis*
Family Hirundinidae (Swallows)
**Size:** 8″
**Season:** Summer in western Colorado; transient elsewhere
**Habitat:** Marshes, open water, agricultural areas

The Purple Martin is the largest North American swallow. It has long, pointed wings, a streamlined body, and a forked tail. The bill is very short and broad at the base. The male is dark overall, with a blackish blue sheen across the back and head, while the female is paler overall, with sooty, mottled underparts. Flight consists of fast wing beats alternating with circular glides. Purple Martins commonly use man-made nest boxes or tree hollows as nesting sites. (Illustration shows an adult male.)

## Northern Rough-winged Swallow,
*Stelgidopteryx serripennis*
Family Hirundinidae (Swallows)
**Size:** 5½″
**Season:** Summer
**Habitat:** Sandy cliffs, riverbanks, outcrops, bridges

The Northern Rough-winged Swallow flies in a smooth and even fashion, with full wing beats, feeding on insects caught on the wing. It is uniform brownish above and white below. The breast is lightly streaked with pale brown, and the tail is short and square. Juveniles show light, rust-colored wing bars on the upper coverts. These fairly solitary swallows find nesting sites in holes in sandy cliffs. (Illustration shows an adult.)

## Violet-green Swallow,
*Tachycineta thalassina*
Family Hirundinidae (Swallows)
**Size:** 5¼"
**Season:** Summer
**Habitat:** Forested areas, especially near water and cliffs

The Violet-green Swallow is a slim, boldly patterned swallow with long wings and a short, notched tail. The wings and tail are dark brown-black, the back is glossy green, and the uppertail coverts and wing coverts are dark purplish. It is pure white underneath, with the white coloring extending to the sides of the rump and up to the face. The top of the head is green. Females are paler and brownish on the back, with gray smudging on the face. Violet-green Swallows are highly aerial and catch small insects on the wing, but will often settle on a perch in plain view. The call includes thin, high-pitched tweets and cheeps. (Illustration shows an adult male.)

## Tree Swallow, *Tachycineta bicolor*
Family Hirundinidae (Swallows)
**Size:** 5¾"
**Season:** Summer
**Habitat:** Variety of habitats near water and perching sites

The Tree Swallow has a short, slightly notched tail, broad-based triangular wings, and a thick neck. It has a high-contrast plumage pattern, with dark, metallic green-blue upperparts and crisp white underparts. When perched, the primaries reach just past the tail tip. Juveniles are gray-brown below, with a subtle, darker breast band. Tree Swallows take insects on the wing but will also eat berries and fruits. The voice is a high-pitched chirping. The swallows often form huge lines of individuals perched on wires or branches. (Illustration shows an adult male.)

## Barn Swallow, *Hirundo rustica*

Family Hirundinidae (Swallows)
**Size:** 6½"
**Season:** Summer
**Habitat:** Old buildings, caves, open rural areas near bridges

The widespread and common Barn Swallow has narrow, pointed wings and a long, deeply forked tail. It is pale below and dark blue above, with a rusty orange forehead and throat. In males the underparts are pale orange, while females are a pale cream color below. Barn Swallows are graceful, fluid fliers, and they often forage in groups to catch insects in flight. The voice is a loud, repetitive chirping or clicking. They build cup-shaped nests of mud on almost any protected man-made structure. (Illustration shows an adult male.)

## Black-capped Chickadee, *Poecile atricapilla*

Family Paridae (Chickadees, Titmice)
**Size:** 5¼"
**Season:** Year-round
**Habitat:** Mixed woodlands, rural gardens, feeders

The Black-capped Chickadee is a small, compact, active bird with short, rounded wings and a tiny, black bill. It is gray above and lighter gray or dusky below, with a contrasting black cap and throat patch. It is quite similar to the eastern Carolina Chickadee, which does not normally occur in Colorado. Its voice sounds like its name—*Chick-A-Dee-Dee-Dee*—or is a soft *Fee-Bay*. It is quite social and feeds on a variety of seeds, berries, and insects found in trees and shrubs. (Illustration shows an adult.)

## Mountain Chickadee,
*Poecile gambeli*
Family Paridae (Chickadees, Titmice)
**Size:** 5¼"
**Season:** Year-round
**Habitat:** Mountainous woodlands

1/28/15

The Mountain Chickadee is a small, fluffy bird with a tiny bill, similar to the Black-capped Chickadee, but with a white superciliary stripe through the black cap. It is grayish above, with pale gray or buff-colored underparts, and has a black crown and chin patch. Energetic and acrobatic, it travels in small groups eating small insects and seeds gleaned from tree branches. Its voice sounds like *Chick-A-Dee-Dee-Dee*. (Illustration shows an adult.)

## Bushtit, *Psaltriparus minimus*
Family Aegithalidae (Bushtits)
**Size:** 4½"
**Season:** Year-round
**Habitat:** Mixed woodlands, scrublands, oaks

The Bushtit is a tiny, ball-shaped, fluffy bird with short, rounded wings, a long tail, and drab plumage. It is brownish gray above and paler gray underneath. The female has a light yellow eye, while that of the male is black. The bill is short and stubby with a curved culmen, and the legs are thin and dark. Bushtits flit from tree to tree in noisy groups, eating berries and insects. The voice is a thin, high-pitched, rapid series of twittering chips. (Illustration shows an adult female.)

## Red-breasted Nuthatch,
*Sitta canadensis*
Family Sittidae (Nuthatches)
**Size:** 4½"
**Season:** Year-round
**Habitat:** Open coniferous and oak forests

The Red-breasted Nuthatch is a small, stubby, large-headed, short-tailed bird with a long, thin, slightly upturned bill. Plumage is blue-gray above and rusty orange or buff colored (in the female) below. The head is white, with a black crown and eye stripe. The nuthatch's legs are short, but its toes are very long to aid in grasping tree bark. Nuthatches creep downward, head first, on tree trunks and branches to pick out insects and seeds. The call is a nasal, repetitive *Yonk, yonk, yonk.* (Illustration shows an adult male.)

## White-breasted Nuthatch,
*Sitta carolinensis*
Family Sittidae (Nuthatches)
**Size:** 5¾"
**Season:** Year-round
**Habitat:** Mixed oak or coniferous woodlands

The White-breasted Nuthatch has a large head and wide neck, short, rounded wings, and a short tail. It is blue-gray above and pale gray below, with rusty smudging on the lower flanks and undertail coverts. The breast and face are white, and there is a black crown merging with the mantle. The bill is long, thin, and upturned at the tip. To forage, it creeps head first down tree trunks to pick out insects and seeds. Its voice is a nasal, repetitive *Auk, auk, auk.* It nests in tree cavities high off the ground. (Illustration shows an adult male.)

### Brown Creeper, *Certhia americana*
Family Certhiidae (Creepers)
**Size:** 5¼"
**Season:** Year-round
**Habitat:** Mature woodlands

The Brown Creeper is a small, cryptically colored bird with a long, pointed tail and a long, down-curved bill. It is mottled black, brown, and white above, and is plain white below, fading to brownish toward the rear. The face has a pale supercilium and a white chin. The legs are short with long, grasping toes. Brown Creepers spiral upward on tree trunks, probing for insects in the bark, then fly to the bottom of another tree to repeat the process. Its stiff tail aids in propping the bird up, like a woodpecker's tail. Its voice is composed of thin, high-pitched *Seet* notes. (Illustration shows an adult.)

WRENS

### House Wren, *Troglodytes aedon*
Family Troglodytidae (Wrens)
**Size:** 4¾"
**Season:** Summer
**Habitat:** Shrubby areas, rural gardens

The House Wren is a loud, drab wren with short, rounded wings and a thin, pointed, down-curved bill. Plumage is brown and barred above, and is pale gray-brown beneath, with barring on the lower belly, undertail coverts, and tail. The head is lighter on the throat, at the lores, and above the eyes. House Wrens feed in the brush for insects, and sing rapid, melodic, chirping songs, often while cocking their tails downward. (Illustration shows an adult.)

**Marsh Wren,** *Cristothorus palustris*
Family Troglodytidae (Wrens)
**Size:** 5"
**Season:** Year-round
**Habitat:** Marshes, reeds, stream banks

The Marsh Wren is a small, cryptic, rufous-brown wren with a normally cocked-up tail. The tail and wings are barred with black, and the chin and breast are white. There is a well-defined white superciliary stripe below a uniform brown crown, and the mantle shows distinct black-and-white striping. The bill is long and slightly decurved. Marsh Wrens are vocal day and night, voicing quick, repetitive cheeping. They are secretive but inquisitive, and glean insects from the marsh vegetation and the water surface. (Illustration shows an adult.)

WRENS

**Rock Wren,** *Salpinctes obsoletus*
Family Troglodytidae (Wrens)
**Size:** 6"
**Season:** Summer; year-round in southwestern Colorado
**Habitat:** Deserts; open, dry, rocky areas

The Rock Wren is stocky, with a short tail, a large head, and a thin, slightly down-curved bill. It is grayish brown above, with fine barring and spotting. Underneath, it is pale buff to gray, with fine streaking along the breast and dark bars on the undertail coverts. There is a pale superciliary stripe above the dark eye. The pale brownish tips of the outer tail feathers are visible when the tail is fanned. Rock Wrens search around rocks for insects, flitting from rock to rock and often bobbing up and down. (Illustration shows an adult.)

### Blue-gray Gnatcatcher,
*Polioptila caerulea*
Family Polioptilidae (Gnatcatchers)
**Size:** 4½"
**Season:** Summer
**Habitat:** Thickets, deciduous or pine woodlands

The Blue-gray Gnatcatcher is a tiny, energetic, long-tailed bird with a narrow, pointed bill and thin, dark legs. It is blue-gray above and pale gray below, with white edges to the tertials creating a light patch on the middle of the folded wing. The tail is rounded and has black inner feathers and white outer feathers. The eyes are surrounded by crisp, white eye rings. Males are brighter blue overall, and have darker supraloral lines. To forage, gnatcatchers flit through thickets and catch insects in the air. They will often twitch and fan their tails. The voice is a high-pitched buzzing or cheep sound, sometimes sounding like the calls of other birds. (Illustration shows an adult male.)

### American Dipper,
*Cinclus mexicanus*
Family Cinclidae (Dippers)
**Size:** 7½"
**Season:** Year-round
**Habitat:** Fast-flowing, rocky, mountainous streams

The American Dipper is an unusual, plump, aquatic songbird with a short tail, long legs, and a short, thin bill. The plumage is dense and usually disheveled, slate gray overall, with a brownish hue on the head. Thin, white crescents are sometimes visible around the dark eyes. Dippers perch on rocks in a stream and plunge into the water, propelled by their wings, to pick out larvae and insects. Sometimes they will use their long toes to cling to underwater rocks. They fly low above the water surface, and course up and down stream corridors. While perched, they constantly bob their bodies up and down. The dipper is also known as the Water Ouzel. (Illustration shows an adult.)

**DIPPERS**

### Ruby-crowned Kinglet,
*Regulus calendula*
Family Regulidae (Kinglets)
**Size:** 4"
**Season:** Summer
**Habitat:** Mixed woodlands, brushy areas

The Ruby-crowned Kinglet in a tiny, plump songbird with a short tail and a diminutive, thin bill. It has a habit of nervously twitching its wings as it actively flits through vegetation gleaning small insects and larvae. It may also hover in search of food. Plumage is pale olive green above and paler below, with patterned wings and pale wing bars on the upper coverts. There are white eye rings, or crescents around the eyes, and the bright red crest of the male bird is only faintly noticeable unless the crest is raised. The voice is a very high-pitched, whistling *Seeee*. (Illustration shows an adult male.)

### Golden-crowned Kinglet,
*Regulus satrapa*
Family Regulidae (Kinglets)
**Size:** 4"
**Season:** Year-round
**Habitat:** Mixed woodlands, brushy areas

The Golden-crowned Kinglet is a tiny, plump songbird with a short tail and a short, pointed bill. It is greenish gray above, with wings patterned in black, white, and green, and pale gray below. The face has a dark eye stripe and crown, and the center of the crown is golden yellow and sometimes raised. The legs are dark with orange toes. Kinglets are in constant motion, flitting and dangling among branches, sometimes hanging upside down or hovering at the edge of branches to feed. Their voice includes very high-pitched *Tzee* notes. (Illustration shows an adult.)

## Townsend's Solitaire,

*Myadestes townsendi*
Family Turdidae (Thrushes)
**Size:** 8½"
**Season:** Year-round
**Habitat:** Mountainous coniferous woodlands, juniper scrub

The Townsend's Solitaire is a slim, elongated thrush with a short, blunt bill. It often perches upright on bare branches with its long tail drooping down. It is grayish overall, darker on the wings and tail, with buff-colored patches at the base of the flight feathers. The eyes are dark with distinctive white eye rings. White outer tail feathers are evident on the fanned tail. The juvenile is darker, with extensive light spotting. Townsend's Solitaires forage for insects, seeds, and pine nuts. (Illustration shows an adult.)

## Mountain Bluebird,

*Sialia currucoides*
Family Turdidae (Thrushes)
**Size:** 7¼"
**Season:** Year-round
**Habitat:** Open mountain meadows, sage land

Compared to other bluebirds, the Mountain Bluebird has a thinner bill, a longer tail, and longer wings. The male is bright, sky blue overall, somewhat paler below, and nearly white at the undertail coverts. The female retains the blue color on the tail and wings, but is pale gray on the back, underparts, and head, with a noticeable white eye ring. Juveniles are similar to females, but darker on the back and spotted below. From perches on branches or posts, Mountain Bluebirds dart out to catch insects. They form large winter flocks and tend to hold their bodies in a horizontal posture. (Illustration shows an adult male.)

## Western Bluebird,
*Sialia mexicana*
Family Turdidae (Thrushes)
**Size:** 7"
**Season:** Year-round in southern Colorado; summer elsewhere
**Habitat:** Open woodland, pastures, fields

The Western Bluebird travels in small groups, feeding on a variety of insects, spiders, and berries. It is stocky, short-tailed, and short-billed, and often perches with an upright posture on wires and posts. The male is brilliant blue above and rusty orange below, with a blue belly and undertail region. The orange extends to the nape, making a subtle collar. The female is paler overall, with a pale throat and eye ring. Juveniles are brownish gray, with extensive white spotting and barred underparts. (Illustration shows a male, below, and a female, above.)

## American Robin,
*Turdus migratorius*
Family Turdidae (Thrushes)
**Size:** 10"
**Season:** Year-round
**Habitat:** Widespread in a variety of habitats, including woodlands, fields, parks, lawns

Familiar and friendly, the American Robin is a large thrush with long legs and a long tail. It commonly holds its head cocked and keeps its wing tips lowered beneath its tail. It is gray-brown above and rufous below, with a darker head and contrasting white eye crescents and loral patches. The chin is streaked black and white, and the bill is yellow with darker edges. Females are typically paler overall, and the juvenile shows spots of white above and dark spots below. Robins forage on the ground, picking out earthworms and insects, or in trees for berries. The robin's song is a series of high, musical phrases, sounding like *Cheery, Cheer-U-Up, Cheerio.* (Illustration shows an adult male.)

THRUSHES

## Hermit Thrush,
*Catharus guttatus*
Family Turdidae (Thrushes)
**Size:** 7"
**Season:** Summer
**Habitat:** Woodlands, brushy areas

The Hermit Thrush is a compact, short-tailed thrush that habitually cocks its tail. It forages on the ground near vegetative cover for insects, worms, and berries, and voices a song of beautiful, flutelike notes. It is reddish to olive brown above, with a rufous tail. Its underparts are white, with dusky flanks and sides and black spotting on the throat and breast. The dark eyes are encircled by white eye rings. In flight the pale wing lining contrasts with the dark flight feathers.

MOCKINGBIRDS, CATBIRDS, THRASHERS

## Gray Catbird, *Dumetella carolinensis*
Family Mimidae (Mockingbirds, Catbirds, Thrashers)
**Size:** 8½"
**Season:** Summer
**Habitat:** Understory at woodland
edges, shrubs, rural gardens

The solitary Gray Catbird is long-necked and sleek, with a sturdy, pointed bill. It is uniformly gray except for its rufous undertail coverts, black crown, and black, rounded tail. It is quite secretive, and spends most of its time hidden in thickets close to the ground, picking through the substrate for insects, berries, and seeds. Its call includes a nasal, catlike *Meew*, from which its name is derived, although it will also mimic the songs of other birds. To escape danger, it will often choose to run away rather than fly. (Illustration shows an adult.)

## Northern Mockingbird,
*Mimus polyglottos*
Family Mimidae (Mockingbirds, Catbirds, Thrashers)
**Size:** 10½"
**Season:** Year-round
**Habitat:** Open fields, grassy areas near vegetative cover, suburbs, parks

The Northern Mockingbird is constantly vocalizing. Its scientific name, *polyglottos,* means "many voices," alluding to its amazing mimicry of the songs of other birds. It is sleek, long-tailed, and long-legged. Plumage is gray above, with darker wings and tail, and off-white to brownish gray below. The bird has two white wing bars, short, dark eye stripes, and pale eye rings. In flight, conspicuous white patches on the inner primaries and coverts and white outer tail feathers can be seen. Like other mimids, the mockingbird forages on the ground for insects and berries, intermittently flicking its wings. (Illustration shows an adult.)

## Brown Thrasher, *Toxostoma rufum*
Family Mimidae (Mockingbirds, Catbirds, Thrashers)
**Size:** 11"
**Season:** Summer in eastern Colorado
**Habitat:** Woodlands, thickets, urban gardens, orchards

The Brown Thrasher is primarily a ground-dwelling bird that thrashes through leaves and dirt for insects and plant material. It has a long tail and legs, and a slightly decurved bill of medium length. Plumage is rufous brown above, including the tail, and whitish below, heavily streaked with brown or black. There are two prominent, pale wing bars, and the outermost corners to the tail are pale. The eyes are yellow to orange. The thrasher's voice includes a variety of musical phrases, often sung from a conspicuous perch. (Illustration shows an adult.)

### Sage Thrasher,
*Oreoscoptes montanus*
Family Mimidae (Mockingbirds, Catbirds, Thrashers)
**Size:** 8½"
**Season:** Summer
**Habitat:** Sagebrush, arid scrublands, junipers

The Sage Thrasher is a relatively small thrasher with a long tail and wings, and a shorter, slightly curved bill. It is brownish gray above, with thin, white bars on the wing coverts. The underside is white or pale buff, with extensive dark streaking. The eyes are bright yellow, and there are white corners to the otherwise dark brown tail. Sage Thrashers run or fly low above the ground when foraging for insects, and they vocalize a variety of melodious warbles, sometimes mimicking other birds. (Illustration shows an adult.)

### European Starling, *Sturnus vulgaris*
Family Sturnidae (Starlings)
**Size:** 8½"
**Season:** Year-round in Colorado
**Habitat:** Almost anywhere, particularly rural fields, gardens, dumps, urban parks

Introduced from Europe, the European Starling has successfully infiltrated most habitats in North America and competes with native birds for nest cavities. It is a stocky, sturdy, aggressive bird that is glossy black overall, with a sheen of green or purple. The breeding adult has a yellow bill and greater iridescence, while the adult in winter is more flat black, with a black bill and numerous white spots. The tail is short and square. Starlings form very large, compact flocks, and fly directly on pointed, triangular wings. The diet of starlings is highly variable and includes insects, grains, and berries. Vocalizations include loud, wheezy whistles and clucks, and imitations of other birdsongs. (Illustration shows a breeding adult.)

## American Pipit,
*Anthus rubescens*
Family Motacillidae (Wagtails, Pipits)
**Size:** 6½"
**Season:** Summer
**Habitat:** Tundra in summer; shoreline beaches and short grassy areas in winter

The American Pipit is a slim, ground-dwelling, sparrow-size bird with long legs and a thin, pointed bill. It is grayish brown above, with pale wing bars, and buff colored or whitish underneath, with variable amounts of dark streaking down the breast, sides, and flanks. The head is gray-brown, with a lighter supercilium and malar area. There are white outer tail feathers on an otherwise dark tail. Pipits walk upright in small groups while foraging for insects on the ground, and often pump and wag their tails. (Illustration shows an adult.)

WAXWINGS

## Cedar Waxwing, *Bombycilla cedrorum*
Family Bombycillidae (Waxwings)
**Size:** 7"
**Season:** Year-round in western Colorado; winter elsewhere
**Habitat:** Woodlands, swamps, urban areas near berry trees

The Cedar Waxwing is a compact, crested songbird with pointed wings and a short tail. Plumage is sleek and smooth, overall brownish gray with paler underparts, a yellowish wash on the belly, and white undertail coverts. The head pattern is striking, with a crisp black mask thinly bordered by white. The tail is tipped with bright yellow. The tips of the secondary feathers are coated with a unique, red, waxy substance. Cedar Waxwings form large flocks and devour berries from one tree, then move on to the next. They may also flycatch small insects. The waxwing's voice is an extremely high-pitched, whistling *Seee.* (Illustration shows an adult.)

### Orange-crowned Warbler,
*Oreothlypis celata*
Family Parulidae (Wood-Warblers)
**Size:** 5"
**Season:** Summer
**Habitat:** Mixed woodlands,
brushy thickets

The Orange-crowned Warbler is rather plain, with a relatively long tail and a thin, pointed bill. It is olive green above and brighter yellow below, streaked with olive, and the undertail coverts are solid yellow. The bird has a short, dark eye line and a thin, pale, broken eye ring. There is much variation in this species, from brighter forms to grayer forms, and the orange crown patch is rarely visible. Orange-crowned Warblers forage for insects or berries in the undergrowth, and voice a long series of descending, staccato *Tit* notes. (Illustration shows an adult.)

### Yellow Warbler, *Dendroica petechia*
Family Parulidae (Wood-Warblers)
**Size:** 5"
**Season:** Summer
**Habitat:** Willows and alders near streamsides,
rural shrubbery, gardens

The Yellow Warbler is widespread in North America, and has a musical voice singing *Sweet-Sweet-Sweet*. It is bright yellow overall, with darker yellow-green coloring above and reddish brown streaking below. The black eyes stand out on its light face, and the bill is relatively thick for a warbler. Clean, yellow stripes are evident on the fanned tail. The female is paler overall, with less noticeable streaking on the breast and sides. Yellow Warblers forage in brush for insects and spiders. (Illustration shows an adult male.)

## Yellow-rumped Warbler,
*Dendroica coronata*
Family Parulidae (Wood-Warblers)
**Size:** 5½"
**Season:** Summer
**Habitat:** Deciduous and coniferous woodlands, suburbs with wax myrtle

Two races of this species occur in North America. The "myrtle" form is dispersed across North America, and the "Audubon's" form is seen west of the Rockies. The "myrtle" variety is blue-gray above, with dark streaks, and white below, with black streaking below the chin and a bright yellow side patch. There is a black mask across the face, bordered by a thin superciliary stripe above and a white throat below. The nonbreeding adult and female are paler, with a more brownish cast to the upperparts. The longish tail has white spots on either side and meets with the conspicuous yellow rump. The "Audubon's" variety has a yellow chin and a gray face. The warblers prefer to eat berries and insects. (Illustration shows an adult male "myrtle" form.)

## Black-throated Gray Warbler,
*Dendroica nigrescens*
Family Parulidae (Wood-Warblers)
**Size:** 5½"
**Season:** Summer
**Habitat:** Oak and pinyon-juniper woodlands, dry pine foothills

The Black-throated Gray Warbler is a boldly patterned, black-and-white warbler with a relatively thick, pointed bill. It is slate gray above, streaked on the mantle, with clear white wing bars. Underneath, it is white, streaked with black that merges into a black throat, and the outer tail feathers are white. The head has white patches below and above the eyes, and there are yellow loral patches. The female has less barring underneath and a black throat. The warblers actively forage through foliage for insects, and voice a series of wheezy notes, ascending in volume, sounding like *Wee-Wee-Wee-Wee-Weet*. (Illustration shows an adult male.)

## American Redstart,
*Setophaga ruticilla*
Family Parulidae (Wood-Warblers)
**Size:** 5"
**Season:** Summer in northern Colorado; spring and fall migrant elsewhere
**Habitat:** Open mixed woodlands in early succession

The constantly active, frenetic American Redstart often fans its tail and wings in display while perched. It is long-tailed, and the plumages of males and females are markedly different. The male is jet black above and white below, with a fiery red patch at the side of its breast and a paler, peachy red color in a wing bar and on the sides of its tail. The female is gray-green above, with a slate gray head and white chin and breast. The colored areas are located on the same parts as on the male, but are yellow. Redstarts eat insects gleaned from branches and bark, or flycatch for insects. (Illustration shows a male, below, and a female, above.)

## Common Yellowthroat,
*Geothlypis trichas*
Family Parulidae (Wood-Warblers)
**Size:** 5"
**Season:** Summer
**Habitat:** Swamps, fields, low vegetation near water

The Common Yellowthroat scampers through the undergrowth looking for insects and spiders in a somewhat wrenlike manner. It is a plump little warbler that often cocks up its tail. Plumage is olive brown above, pale brown to whitish below, with a bright yellow breast/chin region and undertail coverts. The male has a black facial mask trailed by a fuzzy white area on the nape. Females lack the facial mask. (Illustration shows a male, below, and a female, above.)

## MacGillivray's Warbler,
*Oporornis tolmiei*
Family Parulidae (Wood-Warblers)
**Size:** 5¼"
**Season:** Summer
**Habitat:** Woodlands with dense undergrowth; riparian areas

The MacGillivray's Warbler is similar to its eastern counterpart, the Mourning Warbler, but has a slightly longer tail and more prominent white eye arcs. Plumage is olive green above and on the tail, and yellow below, with darker sides and flanks. The head and breast are slate gray, slightly paler in females. They feed on insects, hopping and flitting through the vegetation, sometimes pumping their tails. (Illustration shows an adult male.)

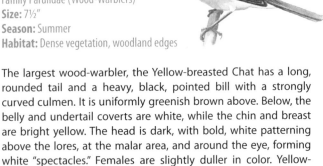

## Yellow-breasted Chat,
*Icteria virens*
Family Parulidae (Wood-Warblers)
**Size:** 7½"
**Season:** Summer
**Habitat:** Dense vegetation, woodland edges

The largest wood-warbler, the Yellow-breasted Chat has a long, rounded tail and a heavy, black, pointed bill with a strongly curved culmen. It is uniformly greenish brown above. Below, the belly and undertail coverts are white, while the chin and breast are bright yellow. The head is dark, with bold, white patterning above the lores, at the malar area, and around the eye, forming white "spectacles." Females are slightly duller in color. Yellow-breasted Chats forage in low brush for insects and berries, and have quite variable vocalizations, including mimicking the songs of other birds. The male has a strange display behavior in which he hovers and dangles his legs. (Illustration shows an adult.)

### Spotted Towhee, *Pipilo maculatus*
Family Emberizidae (Sparrows, Buntings)
**Size:** 8½"
**Season:** Year-round
**Habitat:** Thickets, suburban shrubs, gardens

The Spotted Towhee is a large, long-tailed sparrow with a thick, short bill and sturdy legs. It forages on the ground in dense cover by kicking back both feet at once to uncover insects, seeds, and worms. It is black above, including the head and upper breast, and has rufous sides and a white belly. It has white wing bars, white spotting on the scapulars and mantle, and white corners on the tail. The eye color is red. Females are like the males, but are brown above. The Spotted Towhee was once conspecific with the Eastern Towhee, known as the Rufous-sided Towhee. (Illustration shows an adult male.)

### Chipping Sparrow, *Spizella passerina*
Family Emberizidae (Sparrows, Buntings)
**Size:** 5½"
**Season:** Summer
**Habitat:** Dry fields, woodland edges, gardens

The Chipping Sparrow is a medium-size sparrow with a slightly notched tail and a rounded crest. It is barred black and brown on the upperparts, with a gray rump, and is pale gray below. The head has a rufous crown, white superciliary stripes, dark eye lines, and a white throat. The bill is short, conical, and pointed. Sexes are similar. Winter adults are duller and lack the rufous hue on the crown. Chipping Sparrows feed in trees or on open ground in loose flocks, searching for seeds and insects. The voice is a rapid, staccato chipping sound. (Illustration shows a breeding adult.)

**Lark Bunting,** *Calamospiza melanocorys*
Family Emberizidae (Sparrows, Buntings)
**Size:** 7"
**Season:** Summer
**Habitat:** Open barren grasslands,
arid scrub, sage land

The Colorado state bird, the Lark Bunting is a stocky, distinctive sparrow with a large head, a thick conical bill, a short notched tail, and short wings. It undergoes a dramatic change in plumage during the year. The breeding male is black overall, with a large white patch on the wing coverts. The tail is tipped with white. The nonbreeding male and the female are brownish above, with a pale underside that is extensively streaked with brown. The head is patterned with a white malar patch above a black throat stripe. It forages on the ground for seeds and insects. (Illustration shows a breeding male, below, and a nonbreeding male, above.)

SPARROWS, BUNTINGS

**Lark Sparrow,**
*Chondestes grammacus*
Family Emberizidae (Sparrows,
Buntings)
**Size:** 6½"
**Season:** Summer
**Habitat:** Woodland edges, dry prairies
with brush, agricultural areas

The Lark Sparrow is an elongate, thin sparrow with a long, rounded tail. It is brown above, streaked with dark brown, and white below, with tan around the sides and flanks. There is a distinct dark spot in the middle of the breast. The head is patterned with a rufous crown that has a white medial stripe, rufous cheeks, black eye lines, and a black throat stripe. Lark Sparrows travel in small flocks, hopping or walking on the ground to pick up seeds and insects. They sing a variety of high-pitched chips and trills, often from a conspicuous perch. Males may display with their tails cocked up. (Illustration shows an adult.)

### White-throated Sparrow, *Zonotrichia albicollis*
Family Emberizidae (Sparrows, Buntings)
**Size:** 6½"
**Season:** Spring and fall migrant
**Habitat:** Undergrowth of mixed
woodlands, thickets, gardens

The White-throated Sparrow is a fairly large, round sparrow with a long tail and a typically short, thick bill. It is brown with dark streaking above, has a gray rump, and is grayish below, washed with brown and lightly streaked. The head has a black crown that is bisected by a white medial stripe, white superciliary stripes with yellow near the lores, and dark eye lines. The white chin is sharply bordered by the gray breast below. White-throated Sparrows forage on the ground in small flocks, often with other species, picking up insects and seeds. The sparrow's song is a clean, piercing, simple whistle that mimics the phrase *Old Sam Peabody, Peabody, Peabody.* (Illustration shows an adult.)

### White-crowned Sparrow,
*Zonotrichia leucophrys*
Family Emberizidae (Sparrows,
Buntings)
**Size:** 7"
**Season:** Summer
**Habitat:** Brushy areas, woodland
edges, gardens

The White-crowned Sparrow has a rounded head, sometimes with a raised peak, and a fairly long, slightly notched tail. It is brownish above, streaked on the mantle, and shows pale wing bars. The underside is grayish on the breast, fading to pale brown on the belly and flanks. The head is gray below the eye, and boldly patterned black and white above the eye, with a white medial crown stripe. The bill is bright yellow-orange. White-crowned Sparrows forage on the ground, often in loose flocks, scratching for insects, seeds, and berries. The song is variable, but it usually starts with one longer whistle, followed by several faster notes. (Illustration shows an adult.)

### Song Sparrow, *Melospiza melodia*
Family Emberizidae (Sparrows, Buntings)
**Size:** 6"
**Season:** Year-round
**Habitat:** Thickets, shrubs, woodland edges near water

One of the most common sparrows, the Song Sparrow is fairly plump, with a long, rounded tail. It is brown and gray with streaking above, and white below, with heavy dark or brownish streaking that often congeals into a discreet spot in the middle of the breast. The head has a dark crown with a gray medial stripe, dark eye lines, and a dark malar stripe above the white chin. Song Sparrows are usually seen in small groups or individually, foraging on the ground for insects and seeds. The song is a series of chips and trills of variable pitch, and the call is a *Chip, chip, chip.* (Illustration shows an adult.)

### Dark-eyed Junco,
*Junco hyemalis oreganus*
Family Emberizidae (Sparrows, Buntings)
**Size:** 6½"
**Season:** Winter
**Habitat:** Thickets, rural gardens, open coniferous or mixed woodlands

The Dark-eyed Junco is a small, plump sparrow with a short, conical, pink bill and several distinct variations in plumage. One of the more common races is the "Oregon" Junco, with a rusty brown mantle, sides, and flanks, a white belly, and a black head and breast. Sexes are similar, but the female is paler overall. The white outer tail feathers are obvious in flight. Juncos hop about on the ground, often in groups, picking up insects and seeds. Their voice is a staccato, monotone, chirping trill. Also common in Colorado is the Gray-headed Junco, which is pale gray overall with a rufous mantle. (Illustration shows an adult male of the "Oregon" race.)

## Western Tanager,
*Piranga ludoviciana*
Family Cardinalidae (Tanagers, Cardinals, Grosbeaks)
**Size:** 7¼"
**Season:** Summer
**Habitat:** Mixed or coniferous woodlands

The Western Tanager is a highly arboreal, brightly colored tanager with pointed wings and a short but thick bill. The breeding male has a black upper back, tail, and wings, with a yellow shoulder patch and a white wing bar. The underside and rump are bright yellow, extending across the neck and nape, and the head is red-orange. Females and winter males are paler, with little or no red on the head. Western Tanagers forage for insects, primarily in the upper canopy of mature trees. They are usually difficult to see clearly, but their vocalizations, three-syllabled, rattling high notes with changing accents, are distinctive. (Illustration shows a breeding male.)

## Northern Cardinal,
*Cardinalis cardinalis*
Family Cardinalidae (Tanagers, Cardinals, Grosbeaks)
**Size:** 8½"
**Season:** Year-round in far eastern Colorado
**Habitat:** Woodlands with thickets, suburban gardens

The Northern Cardinal, with its thick, powerful bill, eats mostly seeds but will also forage for fruit and insects. Often found in pairs, they are quite common at suburban feeders. This long-tailed songbird has a thick, short, orange bill and a tall crest. The male is red overall, with a black mask and chin. The female is brownish above and dusky below, crested, and has a dark front to the face. Juveniles are similar to the females but have a black bill. The cardinal's voice is a musical *Weeta-Weeta* or *Woit,* heard from a tall, exposed perch. (Illustration shows a male, below, and a female, above.)

## Black-headed Grosbeak,
*Pheucticus melanocephalus*
Family Cardinalidae (Tanagers, Cardinals, Grosbeaks)
**Size:** 8¼"
**Season:** Summer
**Habitat:** Open woodlands, gardens, riparian areas

The Black-headed Grosbeak is a chunky, large-headed, short-tailed songbird with a massive, thick-based bill that enables it to eat very large seeds. The breeding male is black on the mantle, wings, and tail, with extensive white markings and streaks. The underparts, neck, and rump are rusty orange, with whitish under-tail coverts. The head is black, and the bill is pale on the lower mandible and dark on the upper. The female is brownish above and pale tan below, with darker streaking. The head is brown with a white supercilium and malar patch. Black-headed Grosbeaks eat insects, fruits, and seeds, and sometimes visit feeders. The song consists of erratic, whistling warbles. (Illustration shows a breeding male, below, and a female, above.)

## Blue Grosbeak, *Passerina caerulea*
Family Cardinalidae (Tanagers, Cardinals, Grosbeaks)
**Size:** 6½"
**Season:** Summer
**Habitat:** Woodland edges, thickets, fields

The name "grosbeak" derives from the French word *gros,* meaning "large," and refers to the birds' massive, conical bills. The male Blue Grosbeak is azure blue overall, with rufous wing bars and shoulder patches, black at the front of the face, and a horn-colored bill. The female is brown overall and paler below, with lighter wing bars and lores. The similar Indigo Bunting is smaller, smaller-billed, and lacks the rufous color on the wings. Blue Grosbeaks eat seeds, fruit, and insects in open areas, and habitually flick their tails. They often perch and sing a meandering, warbling song for extended periods. (Illustration shows a male, below, and a female, above.)

### Indigo Bunting,
*Passerina cyanea*
Family Cardinalidae (Tanagers, Cardinals, Grosbeaks)
**Size:** 5½"
**Season:** Summer
**Habitat:** Brushlands, open woodlands, fields

Often occurring in large flocks, the Indigo Bunting forages mostly on the ground for insects, berries, and seeds. It is a small, compact songbird with a short, thick bill. The male is entirely blue, the head being a dark, purplish blue and the body being a lighter, sky blue. The female is brownish gray above and duller below, with faint streaking on the breast meeting a white throat. The winter male is smudged with patchy gray, brown, and white. Indigo Buntings perch in treetops, voicing their undulating, chirping melodies. (Illustration shows a breeding male, below, and a female, above.)

### Western Meadowlark,
*Sturnella neglecta*
Family Icteridae (Blackbirds, Orioles, Grackles)
**Size:** 9½"
**Season:** Year-round
**Habitat:** Open fields, grasslands, meadows

The Western Meadowlark is a chunky, short-tailed icterid with a flat head and a long, pointed bill. It is heavily streaked and barred above, and yellow beneath with dark streaking. The head has a dark crown, white superciliary stripes, dark eye lines, and a yellow chin and malar area. A black, V-shaped necklace that becomes quite pale during winter months is on the upper breast. Nonbreeding plumage is much paler overall. Meadowlarks gather in loose flocks to pick through grasses for insects and seeds. They often perch on telephone wires or posts to sing their short, whistling phrases. (Illustration shows a breeding adult.)

### Bobolink,
*Dolichonyx oryzivorus*
Family Icteridae (Blackbirds, Orioles, Grackles)
**Size:** 7"
**Season:** Summer in northern Colorado
**Habitat:** Lush prairies, grasslands, agricultural areas

BLACKBIRDS, ORIOLES, GRACKLES

The Bobolink is shaped like an elongated sparrow with pointy wings, and exhibits quite different plumage between males and females. The female and winter male are a buff brown overall and paler below, with streaking along the back and sides. On the face is a thin, dark crown and eye stripe. The breeding male is white above and black below, with a two-toned head that is black in front and light yellow in back. The Bobolink's song is a playful, jumbled melody that some compare to its name, *Bobolink-Bobolink*. (Illustration shows a breeding male, below, and a female, above.)

### Brown-headed Cowbird,
*Molothrus ater*
Family Icteridae (Blackbirds, Orioles, Grackles)
**Size:** 7½"
**Season:** Summer
**Habitat:** Woodland edges, pastures with livestock, grassy fields

The Brown-headed Cowbird is a stocky, short-winged, short-tailed blackbird with a short, conical bill. The male is glossy black overall, with a chocolate-brown head, but is sometimes much lighter in western populations. The female is light brown overall, with faint streaking on the underparts and a pale throat. Cowbirds often feed in flocks with other blackbirds, picking seeds and insects from the ground. Vocalizations consist of a number of gurgling, squeaking phrases. Cowbirds practice brood parasitism, whereby they lay their eggs in the nests of other passerine species that then raise their young. Hence, their presence often reduces the populations of other songbirds. (Illustration shows a dark adult male.)

### Yellow-headed Blackbird,
*Xanthocephalus xanthochephalus*
Family Icteridae (Blackbirds, Orioles, Grackles)
**Size:** 9½"; male larger than female
**Season:** Summer
**Habitat:** Farmland, marshy areas with reeds or cattails

The Yellow-headed Blackbird is a large, bold blackbird with a relatively short tail and a deep-based, pointed, triangular bill. The male is black with a bright, golden yellow head and breast. The eyes and lores are black, and there is a white patch on the primary coverts. The female is dark brown, with brown infusing the otherwise yellow head, and white streaking that trickles from the yellow breast. The blackbird's song is a series of raucous, rattling, choking noises, often sung while the bird is perched and fluffing out its feathers. (Illustration shows a male, below, and a female, above.)

### Red-winged Blackbird,
*Agelaius phoeniceus*
Family Icteridae (Blackbirds, Orioles, Grackles)
**Size:** 8½"
**Season:** Year-round
**Habitat:** Marshes, meadows, agricultural areas near water

The Red-winged Blackbird is a widespread, ubiquitous, chunky meadow-dweller that forms huge flocks during the nonbreeding season. The male is deep black overall, with bright orange-red lesser coverts and pale medial coverts that form an obvious shoulder patch in flight but may be partially concealed on the perched bird. The female is barred in tan and dark brown overall, with pale superciliary stripes and a pale malar patch. The blackbirds forage marshland for insects, spiders, and seeds. The voice is a loud, raspy, vibrating *Konk-A-Leee*, given from a perch atop a tall reed or branch. (Illustration shows a male, below, and a female, above.)

### Brewer's Blackbird,
*Euphagus cyanocephalus*
Family Icteridae (Blackbirds, Orioles, Grackles)
**Size:** 9"
**Season:** Year-round
**Habitat:** Meadows, pastures,
open woodlands, urban areas

The Brewer's Blackbird is small-headed and dark, with a short bill and bright yellow eyes (in males). The breeding male is glossy black overall, with purple iridescence on the head and breast, and green iridescence on the wings and tail. During winter the plumage is not as glossy. Females are drab brownish overall, and usually have dark eyes. Brewer's Blackbirds forage on the ground for seeds and insects, often while bowed over with their tails sticking up. The voice is a short, coarse *Zhet,* and a longer, creaky trill. They form large flocks in winter, along with other blackbird species. (Illustration shows a breeding male.)

### Common Grackle,
*Quiscalus quiscula*
Family Icteridae (Blackbirds, Orioles, Grackles)
**Size:** 12½"
**Season:** Summer
**Habitat:** Pastures, open woodlands, urban parks

The Common Grackle is a large blackbird with an elongated body, a long, heavy bill, and a long tail that is fatter toward the tip and is often folded into a keel shape. Plumage is black overall, with a metallic sheen of purple on the head and brown on the wings and underside. The eyes are a contrasting light yellow. Quite social, grackles form huge flocks with other blackbirds and forage on the ground for just about any kind of food, including insects, grains, refuse, and crustaceans. The voice is a high-pitched, rasping trill. (Illustration shows an adult.)

## Bullock's Oriole, *Icterus bullockii*
Family Icteridae (Blackbirds, Orioles, Grackles)
**Size:** 9"
**Season:** Summer
**Habitat:** Deciduous woodlands, suburban gardens, parks

The Bullock's Oriole is flat-crowned and relatively short-tailed with a pointed, broad-based bill. The male is black on the mantle and wings, with a white patch on the wing coverts and white edges to the flight feathers. The body and rump are golden orange, and the head is golden orange with a black chin, black eye lines, and a black crown. The tail is orange with a dark center and tips. Females are gray on the back, pale below, and yellow on the tail, head, and breast. Bullock's Orioles eat insects or berries in the tree canopy and sing in chatterings and chips. The Bullock's Oriole and the Baltimore Oriole are sometimes one species, the Northern Oriole. (Illustration shows a breeding male, below, and a female, above.)

## Evening Grosbeak,
*Coccothraustes vespertinus*
Family Fringillidae (Finches)
**Size:** 8"
**Season:** Year-round
**Habitat:** Coniferous or mixed woodlands, rural gardens

The Evening Grosbeak is a comical-looking finch with a large head, a short stubby tail, and an enormous conical bill. In the male, plumage fades from dark brown on the head to bright yellow toward the rump and belly. The wings are black, with large white patches on the secondaries and tertials. The yellow superciliums merge with the flat forehead and meet the pale, yellow-green bill. The legs are short and pinkish. Females are grayish overall, with choppy white markings on the wings. Evening Grosbeaks travel in flocks to feed on seeds and berries in the upper canopy, and will often visit feeders, preferring sunflower seeds. The voice is a series of short, spaced, rattling *Cheep* notes. (Illustration shows a male, below, and a female, above.)

## Pine Grosbeak,

*Pincola enucleator*
Family Fringillidae (Finches)
**Size:** 9″
**Season:** Year-round, dispersing in winter
**Habitat:** Coniferous forests in mountainous areas

The Pine Grosbeak is a sluggish "winter finch" with a long, slightly notched tail and a large, short bill with a curved culmen and hooked tip. The male is rosy red, with dark wings that have white wing bars and white-edged tertials. The male's sides, flanks, and lower mid-belly are grayish. There is a pale patch of gray below each eye, and minimal dark eye lines. Females are mostly gray, with a light olive green wash across the head, breast, and back. Pine Grosbeaks eat berries, buds, and seeds, and may visit feeders, where they prefer sunflower seeds. Their song is a series of fluty, warbling notes. (Illustration shows a male, below, and a female, above.)

## House Finch,

*Carpodacus mexicanus*
Family Fringillidae (Finches)
**Size:** 6″
**Season:** Year-round
**Habitat:** Woodland edges, urban areas

The House Finch is a western species that has been introduced to eastern North America, and is now common and widespread across the country. It is a relatively slim finch, with a longish, slightly notched tail and a short, conical bill with a down-curved culmen. The male is brown above with streaking on the back, and pale below with heavy streaking. An orange-red wash pervades the supercilium, throat, and upper breast. The female is a drab gray-brown, with similar streaking on the back and underside, and no red on the face or breast. House Finches have a variable diet that includes seeds, insects, and fruit, and they are often the most abundant birds visiting feeders. The voice is a rapid, musical warble. (Illustration shows an adult male.)

## Pine Siskin, *Spinus pinus*
Family Fringillidae (Finches)
**Size:** 5"
**Season:** Year-round
**Habitat:** Coniferous woodlands, rural gardens

The Pine Siskin is a small, cryptically colored finch with a short tail and a narrow, pointed bill. The head and back are light brown overall, heavily streaked with darker brown. The underside is whitish and streaked in darker shades. There is a prominent yellow wing bar on the greater coverts, and yellow on the flight feather edges and at the base of the primaries. Females are marked similarly, with a darker underside and white—not yellow—wing bars. Individuals can be quite variable as to the amount of streaking and the prominence of the yellow coloring. Pine Siskins forage energetically in small groups for seeds and insects, sometimes clinging upside down on twigs to reach food. Their voice consists of high-pitched, erratic, raspy chips and trills. (Illustration shows an adult male.)

## American Goldfinch,
*Spinus tristis*
Family Fringillidae (Finches)
**Size:** 5"
**Season:** Year-round
**Habitat:** Open fields, marshes, urban feeders

The American Goldfinch is a small, cheerful, social finch with a short, notched tail and a small, conical bill. In winter it is brownish gray, lighter underneath, with black wings and tail. There is bright yellow on the shoulders, around the eyes, and along the chin, along with two white wing bars. In breeding plumage the male becomes light yellow across the back, underside, and head, and develops a black forehead and loreal area. Also, the bill becomes orange. Females look similar to the males in winter plumage. Goldfinches forage by actively searching for insects and seeds of all kinds, particularly thistle seeds. The voice is a meandering, musical warble that includes high *Cheep* notes. (Illustration shows a breeding male, below, and a female, above.)

# House Sparrow,
*Passer domesticus*
Family Passeridae (Old World Sparrows)
**Size:** 6¼"
**Season:** Year-round
**Habitat:** Urban environments,
rural pastures

Introduced from Europe, the House Sparrow is ubiquitous in almost every city in the United States, and is often the only sparrow-type bird seen in urban areas. It is stocky, aggressive, and gregarious, and has a relatively large head and a short, finchlike bill. Males are streaked brown and black above, and pale below. The lores, chin, and breast are black, while the crown and auriculars are gray. There are prominent white wing bars at the medial coverts. In winter the male lacks the dark breast patch. Females are drab overall, with a lighter bill and pale supercilium. House Sparrows have a highly varied diet, including grains, insects, berries, and crumbs from the local cafe. The voice is a series of rather unmusical chirps. (Illustration shows a breeding male, below, and a female, above.)

# Index

# About the Author and Illustrator

Todd Telander is a naturalist, illustrator, and artist living in Walla Walla, Washington. He has studied and illustrated wildlife since 1989, while living in California, Colorado, New Mexico, and Washington state. He graduated from the University of California at Santa Cruz with degrees in biology, environmental studies, and scientific illustration, and has illustrated numerous  books and other publications, including FalconGuides' Scats and Tracks series. His work can be viewed online at www.toddtelander .com.